"This book is vintage DeYoung—ruthlessly biblical."

John Piper, Pastor for Preaching and Vision, Bethlehem Baptist Church, Twin Cities, Minnesota

"My heart resonated deeply when I first heard Kevin speak on this subject. His message is a wake-up call to God's people—timely, prophetic, and desperately needed in our day. As a gifted theologian and thinker, Kevin tackles many of the biblical intricacies and nuances of true holiness. As a pastor, he evidences sincere compassion and concern for the condition of the flock. As a fellow pilgrim, he gets to the heart of ways of thinking and living that keep us from reflecting our holy God in this dark world. As a servant and lover of Christ, he holds out a vision of the beauty and power of personal holiness."

Nancy Leigh DeMoss, author, *Revive Our Hearts* radio host

"Holiness was once a central component of following Christ. But for many today, the Christian life is little more than a celebration of cheap grace and pseudo-liberty, with a high tolerance for sin. In this well-written and much-needed book, Kevin DeYoung thoughtfully points us to an unpopular yet strangely liberating truth—that God is holy and expects *us* to be holy. With no hint of legalism or drudgery, Kevin offers a balanced and engaging view of law and grace. Kevin DeYoung is one of my favorite writers, and this book demonstrates why. I repeatedly said 'Yes!' as I turned these pages. I'm convinced that Christ-followers desperately need to read, discuss, and live out the timely, God-exalting message of *The Hole in Our Holiness*!"

Randy Alcorn, founder and director, Eternal Perspective Ministries; author, *If God Is Good* and *Heaven*

"Grace is too amazing to save us from sin's guilt only to leave us under its cruel tyranny. In this book, Kevin DeYoung reminds us that the gospel is the ground of our justification and sanctification. At the same time, he reminds us of the many exhortations in Scripture to pursue godliness as the fruit of our union with Christ in the power of the Spirit. *The Hole in Our Holiness* offers important reflections on a crucial topic in the ongoing conversation about the joys and struggles of the Christian life."

Michael Horton, Professor of Theology, Westminster Seminary California; author, *The Christian Faith: A Systematic Theology for Pilgrims on the Way*

"One might expect a book about holiness to be heavy on finger-pointing, leaning toward legalism, and embarrassingly out-of-touch. But *The Hole in Our Holiness* is none of those things. Instead, Kevin DeYoung gets specific about what Spirit-infused, gospel-driven effort toward holiness looks like. Going way past 'try harder' and 'believe better,' this book implants in readers not just a longing to be holy but real hope that it could happen."

Nancy Guthrie, author of the Seeing Jesus in the Old Testament Bible study series

"J. C. Ryle wrote his classic *Holiness* out of a concern that 'practical holiness and entire consecration to God are not sufficiently attended to by modern Christians in this country.' It is with the same prescient concern and pastoral insight that my friend Kevin DeYoung has written what I consider to be the modern equivalent, urging a new generation of Christians to obey God's command to 'be holy, for I am holy.' May *The Hole in Our Holiness* do for our time what *Holiness* did in a previous age: promote gospel-centered holiness in Christians and churches around the world."

C. J. Mahaney, Sovereign Grace Ministries

"The strength of this book lies in its biblical understanding that all great renewal is founded upon knowing the goodness and holiness of God. We are commanded to be holy because he is holy, and only in Christ can we be trained accordingly: 'For the grace of God has appeared bringing salvation to all people, training us to renounce ungodliness and worldly passions, and to live self-controlled, upright, and godly lives in the present age' (Titus 2:11). I pray that Kevin's words would be read widely and that the church might be known as a people 'zealous for good works' upon seeing the Father's holiness and Christ's redeeming work."

John M. Perkins, President, John M. Perkins Foundation for Reconciliation and Development

"I have loved being under Kevin's teaching during my college years, specifically on this matter of holiness. This is indispensable reading material for all who desire a life of piety. Though we are fallen people, Kevin points us to our potential for godliness and how our progress in this area is of the utmost importance. Get your highlighter ready!"

Kirk Cousins, former starting quarterback, Michigan State University; quarterback, Washington Redskins

THE

H●LE

IN ●UR

H●LINESS

Filling the Gap between Gospel Passion
and the Pursuit of Godliness

KEVIN DEYOUNG

CROSSWAY
WHEATON, ILLINOIS

The Hole in Our Holiness: Filling the Gap between Gospel Passion and the Pursuit of Godliness

Copyright © 2012 by Kevin DeYoung

Published by Crossway
          1300 Crescent Street
          Wheaton, Illinois 60187

Published in association with the literary agency of Wolgemuth & Associates, Inc.

Cover design: Josh Dennis

First printing 2012

Printed in the United States of America

Trade Paperback ISBN: 978-1-4335-4135-3
PDF ISBN: 978-1-4335-3335-8
Mobipocket ISBN: 978-1-4335-3336-5
EPub ISBN: 978-1-4335-3337-2

Library of Congress Cataloging-in-Publication Data

   DeYoung, Kevin.
The hole in our holiness : filling the gap between Gospel pas-
sion and the pursuit of godliness / Kevin DeYoung.
     p. cm.
Includes indexes.
   ISBN 978-1-4335-3334-1 (hc)
   1. Christian life. 2. Holiness—Christianity. I. Title.
BV4509.5.D49   2012
248.8'44—dc23   2012001371

Crossway is a publishing ministry of Good News Publishers.

LB		24	23	22	21	20	19	18	17	16	15
16	15	14	13	12	11	10	9	8	7	6	5	4	3

To the elders and pastors at
University Reformed Church,
with gratitude for their hard work
and their pursuit of holiness.

CONTENTS

Chapter One

MIND THE GAP

I've never understood the attraction of camping. Although I have plenty of friends and relatives who are avid campers, it's always seemed strange to me that someone would work hard all year so they can go live outside for a week. I get the togetherness stuff, but why do it in tents with community toilets? As an adventure, I sort of understand camping. You strap a pack on your back and go hike God's creation. Cool. But packing up the van like Noah's ark and driving to a mosquito infested campground where you reconstitute an inconvenient version of your kitchen and your bedroom just doesn't make sense. Who decided that vacation should be like normal life, only harder?

Every year our church advertises "family camp." Every year my wife wants to go, and every year we surprisingly end up in some other state during our church's allotted week. As best I can tell, the appeal of family camp is that the kids, unbothered by parental involvement, run around free and dirty sunup to sundown—a sort of *Lord of the Flies* for little Michiganders. But as appealing as it sounds to have absentee offspring and downtime with my friends, there must be a cleaner, less humid way to export the children for a week (isn't that what VBS is for?). And even if the kids have a great time, the weather holds up, no one needs stitches, and the seventeenth hot dog tastes as good as the first, it will still be difficult to get all the sand out of my books.

I know there are a lot of die-hard campers in the world. I

don't fault you for your hobby. It's just not my thing. I didn't grow up camping. My family wasn't what you'd call "outdoorsy." We weren't against the outdoors or anything. We often saw it through our windows and walked through it on our way to stores. But we never once went camping. We didn't own a tent, an RV, or Fifth Wheel. No one hunted. No one fished. Even our grill was inside (seriously, a Jenn-Air; look it up).

I've been largely ignorant of camping my whole life. And I'm okay with that. It's one more thing I don't need to worry about in life. Camping may be great for other people, but I'm content to never talk about it, never think about it, and never do it. Knock yourself out with the cooler and collapsible chairs, but camping is not required of me, and I'm fine without it.

HOLINESS IS THE NEW CAMPING

Is it possible you look at personal holiness like I look at camping? It's fine for other people. You sort of respect those who make their lives harder than they have to be. But it's not really your thing. You didn't grow up with a concern for holiness. It wasn't something you talked about. It wasn't what your family prayed about or your church emphasized. So, to this day, it's not your passion. The pursuit of holiness feels like one more thing to worry about in your already impossible life. Sure, it would be great to be a better person, and you do hope to avoid the really big sins. But you figure, since we're saved by grace, holiness is not required of you, and frankly, your life seems fine without it.

The hole in our holiness is that we don't really care much about it. Passionate exhortation to pursue gospel-driven holiness is barely heard in most of our churches. It's not that we don't talk about sin or encourage decent behavior. Too many sermons are basically self-help seminars on becoming a better you. That's moralism, and it's not helpful. Any gospel which says only what you *must do* and never announces what Christ *has done* is no gospel at all. So I'm not talking about getting beat up every Sunday for watching *SportsCenter* and driving an SUV. I'm talking about the failure of Christians, especially younger generations and especially those most disdainful of "religion" and "legalism," to take seriously one of the great aims of our redemption and one of the required evidences for eternal life—our holiness.

J. C. Ryle, a nineteenth-century Bishop of Liverpool, was right: "We must be holy, because *this is one grand end and purpose* for which Christ came into the world. . . . Jesus is a complete Saviour. He does not merely take away the guilt of a believer's sin, he does more—he breaks its power (1 Pet. 1:2; Rom. 8:29; Eph. 1:4; 2 Tim. 1:9; Heb. 12:10)."[1] My fear is that as we rightly celebrate, and in some quarters rediscover, all that Christ has saved us *from*, we are giving little thought and making little effort concerning all that Christ has saved us *to*. Shouldn't those most passionate about the gospel and God's glory also be those most dedicated to the pursuit of godliness? I worry that there is an enthusiasm gap and no one seems to mind.

WHO SAYS?

How do I know there is a hole in our holiness? Well, I don't. Who can possibly assess the state of the evangelical church or the church in North America, let alone the church around the globe? I could give you statistics about pastoral meltdowns or figures about the worldliness of the average churchgoer. You've probably seen them before and paid little attention. Anyone can say anything with statistics. Seventy-three percent of registered voters know that.

---

[1]J. C. Ryle, *Holiness: Its Nature, Hindrances, Difficulties, and Roots* (Moscow, ID: Charles Nolan, 2011), 49 (emphasis mine).

So I make no claim to have scientifically proven that Christians are neglecting the pursuit of holiness. But I'm not the first to think there is something missing in the contemporary church scene. In his book *Rediscovering Holiness*, J. I. Packer claims that present-day believers find holiness passé.[2] He cites three pieces of evidence: (1) We do not hear about holiness in preaching and books. (2) We do not insist upon holiness in our leaders. (3) We do not touch upon the need for personal holiness in our evangelism. These observations sound right to me.

But if you don't want to take Packer's word for it, think about these three diagnostic questions based on three passages of Scripture:

1. Is Our Obedience Known to All?

In most of Paul's letters he gives his churches a lot of encouragement. He usually begins by saying something like, "I'm so thankful for you. You guys are awesome. I think about you all the time, and when I do, it makes me praise God." He's a proud spiritual papa. But he wasn't passing out "My Christian is an honor roll saint at the Apostolic School for the Gifted" bumper stickers. He didn't have to. Others noticed for themselves. In Romans 16:19, for example, Paul says, "your obedience is known to all." Granted, reputations can be wrong (Rev. 3:1), and the Romans had their own issues to work out. But this commendation at the end of Romans forces us to ask the question: Is obedience what your church is known for? Is it what other Christians think of when they look at your life? Is this even what you would want to be known for? "Creativity" or "relevance" or "world-changer" might sound better than boring old obedience.

---

[2] J. I. Packer, *Rediscovering Holiness: Know the Fullness of Life with God* (Ventura, CA: Regal, 2009), 31–32.

I'm challenged by the Puritans in this regard. I know you might hear "Puritan" and imagine a perpetual party-pooper who "has a sneaking suspicion that someone somewhere is having a good time."[3] But the real Puritans were not like that. They enjoyed God's good gifts while at the same time pursuing godliness as among God's greatest gifts. That's why one theologian described Puritanism as a Reformed holiness movement.[4] They were fallible but Bible-believing Christians passionate in their pursuit of God and godliness. Puritan spirituality was not focused on spiritual gifts, or experience for its own sake, or losing oneself in a mysterious cloud of unknowing. Puritan spirituality was about growing in holiness. It was about Christians becoming visible saints. That's why they defined theology as "the doctrine of living to God" (William Ames) or "the science of living blessedly forever" (William Perkins).[5] Their passion and prayer was for holiness. Can we honestly say our lives and our churches are marked by the same pursuit?

2. Is Our Heaven a Holy Place?

In Revelation 21 we get a stunning glimpse of the new heaven and new earth. While most Christians are naturally curious about this recreated world, the Bible doesn't actually give a lot of specifics. But what we do know is what we really need to know. The new Jerusalem is glorious—it shines with the radiance of God's presence. The new Jerusalem is safe—there is no more suffering, no more chaotic sea, and no more closed gates (because there are no more enemies). And most importantly for our purposes, the new

---

[3]Attributed to H. L. Mencken.
[4]Richard Lovelace, "Afterword: The Puritans and Spiritual Renewal," in *The Devoted Life: An Invitation to the Puritan Classics*, ed. Kelly M. Kapic and Ronald C. Gleason (Downers Grove, IL: InterVarsity Press, 2004), 301.
[5]Ibid.

Jerusalem is holy—not only has the bride been purified but the dimensions of the city suggest that heaven is a reconstituting of the Holy of Holies.

In some popular conceptions of the afterlife, God's love gets reduced to unconditional affirmation. But in truth, God's love is always a holy love and his heaven is an entirely holy place. Heaven is for those who conquer, for those who overcome the temptation to abandon Jesus Christ and compromise their faith (Rev. 21:7; see also Revelation 2–3). "But," Revelation 21:8 goes on to say, "as for the cowardly, the faithless, the detestable, as for murderers, the sexually immoral, sorcerers, idolaters, and all liars, their portion will be in the lake that burns with fire and sulfur, which is the second death." No matter what you profess, if you show disregard for Christ by giving yourself over to sin—impenitently and habitually—then heaven is not your home.

Do you know why so many Christians are caving on the issue of homosexuality? Certainly cultural pressure plays a big role. But our failure to really understand the holiness of heaven is another significant factor. If heaven is a place of universal acceptance for all pretty nice people, why should anyone make a big deal about homosexuality here on earth? Many Christians have never been taught that sorcerers and murderers and idolaters and everyone who loves and practices falsehood will be left outside the gates of heaven (Rev. 22:15). So they do not have the guts (or the compassion) to say that the unrepentantly sexually immoral will not be welcomed in either, which is exactly what Revelation 21–22 teaches.

Because God's new world is free from every stain or hint of sin, it's hard to imagine how we could enjoy heaven without holiness. As J. C. Ryle reminds us, heaven is a holy place. The Lord of heaven is a holy God. The angels are holy creatures. The inhabitants are holy saints. Holiness is written on everything in heaven. And nothing unholy can enter into this heaven (Rev. 21:27; Heb. 12:14). Even if you could enter heaven without holiness, what would you do? What joy would you feel there? What holy man or woman of God would you sit down with for fellowship? Their pleasures are not your pleasures. Their character is not your character. What they love, you do not love. If you dislike a holy God now, why would you want to be with him forever? If worship does not capture your attention at present, what makes you think it will thrill you in some heavenly future? If ungodliness is your delight here on earth, what will please you in heaven, where all is clean and pure? You would not be happy there if you are not holy here.[6] Or as Spurgeon put it, "Sooner could a fish live upon a tree than the wicked in Paradise."[7]

3. Are We Great Commission Christians?

Here's a quick quiz: summarize the Great Commission Jesus gives at the end of Matthew 28. If you don't know what that is, go ahead and look it up. But if you know what I'm talking about, think of your two-sentence summary. Don't quote the verses; just put them in your own words. What does Jesus commission us to do in the Great Commission?

You may have said, "He sends us into the world to evangelize." Or maybe you said, "He wants us to preach the gospel to the nations." Or perhaps you said something about making disciples. Those aren't wrong answers. But do you recall Jesus' precise instructions? "Go therefore and make disciples of all nations, baptizing them in the name of the Father and of the Son and of the Holy

---

[6]This paragraph is a summary of Ryle, *Holiness*, 53.
[7]This quote comes from Spurgeon's commentary on Psalm 1:5 in *The Treasury of David*, which can be found online in numerous places, including http://www.spurgeon.org/treasury/ps001.htm.

Spirit, *teaching them to observe all that I have commanded you*" (Matt. 28:19–20a). The word "observe" means more than "take notice of." It means "obey." We aren't asking the nations to look at Jesus' commands like an interesting Rembrandt. We are teaching the nations to follow his commands. The Great Commission is about holiness. God wants the world to know Jesus, believe in Jesus, *and* obey Jesus. We don't take the Great Commission seriously if we don't help each other grow in obedience.

And yet, how many of us usually think of holiness when we think of mission work? How easy it is to be content with leading people to make decisions for Christ instead of focusing on making disciples of Christ. Of course, this doesn't mean we are merely trying to make good people who live like Jesus. The Great Commission would mean nothing and accomplish nothing were it not for the fact that the one who issued it has "all authority in heaven and on earth" (Matt. 28:18). It is only by trusting in him and being forgiven by his substitutionary sacrifice that we are even capable of walking in his ways. You can't make good fruit grow from bad trees. The demands of Jesus cannot be separated from his person and work. Whatever holiness he requires is as the fruit of his redeeming work and for the display of his personal glory.[8] But in all this necessary nuance, do not miss what many churches have overlooked: Jesus expects obedience from his disciples. Passing on the imperatives of Christ is at the heart of the Great Commission.

WHY SO HOLEY?

Everything up to this point begs the question "Why?" Or better yet, "Where?" Where did we get this hole in our holiness? If God's

---

[8]These last two sentences paraphrase John Piper, *What Jesus Demands from the World* (Wheaton, IL: Crossway, 2006), 23.

mission in the world is to save unholy people and to sanctify those he saves, if God justifies the ungodly through faith alone and then promises to make the faithful godly, if the Holy One of Israel is in the business of making a holy people for himself—then why does it seem unlikely that any of us are part of a denomination or ministry network or affiliation of friends that has recently been described as any kind of "holiness movement"? Remember, the Puritans (*pure*-itans) did not invent that name for themselves. Their opponents coined the term because they thought the Puritans were so intensely focused on being, well, pure. The pursuit of holiness does not occupy the place in our hearts that it did in theirs. More critically, a concern for holiness is not obvious in our lives like it's obvious in the pages of Scripture. So why is that? Where did the hole come from?

For starters, it was too common in the past to equate holiness with abstaining from a few taboo practices such as drinking, smoking, and dancing. Godliness meant you avoided the no-no list. Younger generations have little patience for these sorts of rules. In some cases they don't agree with the rules (e.g., about movies, dancing, gambling). In other instances the rules just seem easy to manage. I know when I was growing up it seemed like holiness meant no alcohol, no drugs, and no sex. I wouldn't have known how to get drugs if I tried. Beer smelled bad. And there sure as shootin' wasn't a long line of girls itching to get close to me. So I felt pretty good.

Related to this first reason is the fear that a passion for holiness makes you some kind of weird holdover from a bygone era. As soon as you share your concern about swearing or about avoiding certain movies or about modesty or sexual purity or self-control or just plain godliness, people look at you like you have a moralistic dab of cream cheese on your face from the 1950s. Believers get nervous that their friends will call them legalistic, prudish, narrow-minded, old fashioned, holier-than-thou—or worst of all, a fundamentalist.

Another reason for the hole is that our churches have many unregenerate persons in them. While I don't want genuine Christians to walk away from this book questioning their assurance, I do anticipate (and hope) that some professing believers will come to see they haven't really put their trust in Christ. One reason God's holy people do not pursue holiness is that they have not yet been born again by the Holy Spirit. Some pollsters and pundits look at the worldliness of the church and conclude that being born again doesn't make a difference in how people live. We should come to the opposite conclusion; namely, that many churchgoers are not truly born again.[9] As A. W. Tozer put it, "Plain horse sense ought to tell us that anything that makes no change in the man who professes it makes no difference to God either, and it is an easily observable fact that for countless numbers of persons the change from no-faith to faith makes no actual difference in the life."[10]

Our culture of cool is also partly to blame. To be cool means you differentiate yourself from others. That often means pushing the boundaries with language, with entertainment, with alcohol, and with fashion. Of course, holiness is much more than these things, but in an effort to be hip, many Christians have figured holiness has *nothing* to do with these things. They've willingly embraced Christian freedom but without an equal pursuit of Christian virtue.

Among more liberal Christians, the pursuit of holiness can be suspect because labeling any behavior as "ungodly" feels judgmen-

---

[9]See John Piper, *Finally Alive* (Fearn, Ross-shire, UK: Christian Focus, 2009).
[10]A. W. Tozer, *The Best of A. W. Tozer, Volume 1* (Grand Rapids, MI: Baker, 1978), 168.

tal and intolerant. If we are to be "without spot or blemish" (see Eph. 5:27), we need to discern what sort of attitudes, actions, and habits are pure and what sort are impure. This sort of sorting gets you in trouble with the pluralism police.

Among conservative Christians there is sometimes the mistaken notion that if we are truly gospel-centered we won't talk about rules or imperatives or moral exertion. We are so eager not to confuse indicatives (what God has done) and imperatives (what we should do) that we get leery of letting biblical commands lead uncomfortably to conviction of sin. We're scared of words like diligence, effort, and duty. Pastors don't know how to preach the good news in their sermons and still strongly exhort churchgoers to cleanse themselves from every defilement of body and spirit (2 Cor. 7:1). We know legalism (salvation by law keeping) and antinomianism (salvation without the need for law keeping) are both wrong, but antinomianism feels like a much safer danger.

Then there's the reality that holiness is plain hard work, and we're often lazy. We like our sins, and dying to them is painful. Almost everything is easier than growing in godliness. So we try and fail, try and fail, and then give up. It's easier to sign a petition protesting man's inhumanity to man than to love your neighbor as yourself. It's one thing to graduate from college ready to change the world. It's another to be resolute in praying that God would change you.

And finally, many Christians have simply given up on sanctification. I frequently hear from believers who doubt that holiness is even possible. And it's not just because the process is difficult. It's because we imagine God to be difficult. If our best deeds are nothing but filthy rags (Isa. 64:6, KJV), why bother? We are all hopeless sinners. We can do nothing to please God. No one is really humble or pure or obedient. The pursuit of holiness is just bound to make us feel guilty. So we figure all we can really do is cling to Christ. We are loved because of the imputed righteousness of Christ, but personal obedience that pleases God is simply not possible. The truly super-spiritual do not "pursue holiness"; they celebrate their failures as opportunities to magnify the grace of God.

BUT HE (MAY) HAVE THIS AGAINST YOU

I see a growing number of Christians today eager to think about creative ways to engage the culture. It's not hard to find Christians fired up about planting churches and kingdom work. You can even find lots of believers passionate about precise theology. Yes and Amen to all that. Seriously. There's no need to tear down what is good and true just because something else good and true may be missing. Jesus commended the churches in Revelation where they were faithful and then challenged them where they were in spiritual danger. I have no interest in making anyone feel bad for being passionate about Bach, bass fishing, or Herman Bavinck. There are a hundred good things you may be called to pursue as a Christian. All I'm saying is that, according to the Bible, holiness, for every single Christian, should be right at the top of that list. We need more Christians on our campuses, in our cities, in our churches, and in our seminaries who will say with Paul, "Look carefully then how you walk" (Eph. 5:15).

Is it possible that with all the positive signs of spiritual life in your church or in your heart, there is still a sad disregard for your own personal holiness? When was the last time we took a verse like, "Let there be no filthiness nor foolish talk nor crude joking, which are out of place, but instead let there be thanksgiving" (Eph. 5:4) and even began to try to apply this to our conversation, our movies, our YouTube clips, our television and commercial intake? What does it mean that there must not be even a hint of immorality among the saints (v. 3)? It must mean something. In our sex-saturated culture, I would be surprised if there were not at least a few hints of immorality in our texts and tweets and inside jokes. And what about our clothes, our music, our flirting, and the way we talk about people who aren't in the room? If the war on poverty is worth fighting, how much more the war on your own sin? The fact of the matter is, if you read through the instructions to the New Testament churches you will find few explicit commands that tell us to take care of the needy in our communities and no explicit commands to do creation care, but there are dozens and dozens of verses that enjoin us, in one way or another, to be holy as God is holy (e.g., 1 Pet. 1:13–16).

Let me say it again: I do not wish to denigrate any of the other biblical emphases capturing the attention of churches and Christians today. I know it makes a more exciting book if I say everyone else has missed the boat. That's not the case, however. The sky is not falling, and it won't until Jesus falls from it first. But we don't have to pretend everything else is wrong to recognize we don't have everything right. There is a gap between our love for the gospel and our love for godliness. This must change. It's not pietism, legalism, or fundamentalism to take holiness seriously. It's the way of all those who have been called to a holy calling by a holy God.

Chapter Two

THE REASON FOR REDEMPTION

Why did God save you?

It's not a bad question, if you think about it. After all, you were dead in your sins and trespasses (Eph. 2:1). As a descendent of the first man, Adam, you share in the guilt and corruption of his, the first sin (Rom. 5:12–21). You were an enemy of God (v. 10), a sinner brought forth in iniquity (Ps. 51:5), by nature deserving of wrath (Eph. 2:3). You were a sinner who sinned and deserved to die (Rom. 6:23). But here's the good news for every Christian reading this book: the Bible says that, at just the right time, Jesus Christ died for you (5:8). The Good Shepherd laid down his life for his sheep (John 10:15). Jesus drank the cup of God's wrath for you (see Mark 10:45). His death on the cross means God is now for you instead of against you (Rom. 3:25; 8:31–39). By faith, through the life, death, and resurrection of Christ, you are a reconciled, justified, adopted child of God. What good news!

But why?

Maybe you've thought about *how* God saves us, or *what* we must do to be saved, or *when* you were saved. But have you ever considered *why* he saved you?

There is more than one right answer to that question. The Bible says God saved us because he loves us (John 3:16). It also tells us that God saved us for the praise of his own name (Eph. 1:6, 12, 14). Those are two of the best answers to the why question.

But there is another answer—just as good, just as biblical, just as important. God saved you so that you might be holy. Pay attention to the purpose statement in this passage from Ephesians:

> Blessed be the God and Father of our Lord Jesus Christ, who has blessed us in Christ with every spiritual blessing in the heavenly places, even as he chose us in him . . . *that we should be holy and blameless* before him. (Eph. 1:3–4)

God chose us for salvation in eternity past and sent Christ to save us in history and gave us the gift of faith by the working of the Holy Spirit in our lifetimes *so that* we might be holy.

And notice Paul is not talking about the righteousness of Christ reckoned to our account when we believe in Jesus. I'll have much more to say about this in the pages ahead, but I want you to see from the outset that Ephesians 1:4 (and there are lots of texts like this one) is talking about a personal holiness that must characterize the life of the believer on the last day and at the present time.[1] Paul is setting up the summons to put off the old self and put on the new (4:22–24). He's thinking of being cleansed by the washing of water with the word (5:26). When God saves us by the righteousness of Christ, he saves us so that we too should be marked by righteousness. As J. I. Packer put it, "In reality, holiness is the goal of our redemption. As Christ died in order that we may be justified, so we are justified in order that we may be sanctified and made holy."[2]

---

[1] Peter T. O'Brien, after arguing that Ephesians 1:4 looks forward to the final acquittal on the last day, adds, "But this is not to suggest that there is consequently no concern for holiness and blamelessness in the here and now. The 'holiness without which no one will see the Lord' (Heb. 12:14) is progressively wrought within the lives of the believers on earth by the Spirit, and will be consummated in glory at the *parousia*, the time of the 'redemption' anticipated in Eph. 1:14; 4:30. And the clear implication for believers is that even now they should live according to the divine intention" (*The Letter to the Ephesians* [Grand Rapids, MI: Eerdmans, 1999], 100).

[2] J. I. Packer, *Rediscovering Holiness: Know the Fullness of Life with God* (Ventura, CA: Regal, 2009), 33.

Distinctive holiness has been God's plan for his people in both Testaments:

> You yourselves have seen what I did to the Egyptians, and how I bore you on eagles' wings and brought you to myself. Now therefore, if you will indeed obey my voice and keep my covenant, you shall be my treasured possession among all peoples, for all the earth is mine; and you shall be to me a kingdom of priests and a holy nation. (Ex. 19:4–6a)

Do you see again the reason for divine deliverance? God saved the Israelites *unto* holiness. God set them free from slavery to the Egyptians so they might be free to walk in his ways. They were to be a nation of people so set apart, so sanctified, so holy that they might as well have been priests—every last one of them. Every Christian in every church ought to live out this same priestly identity (1 Pet. 2:9). It's the reason God has rescued us:

- "Therefore do not be ashamed of the testimony about our Lord, nor of me his prisoner, but share in suffering for the gospel by the power of God, *who saved us and called us to a holy calling*, not because of our works but because of his own purpose and grace, which he gave us in Christ Jesus before the ages began" (2 Tim. 1:8–9).
- "For God has not called us for impurity, but in holiness" (1 Thess. 4:7).
- "For we are his workmanship, created in Christ Jesus for good works, which God prepared beforehand, that we should walk in them" (Eph. 2:10).
- "Husbands, love your wives, as Christ loved the church and gave himself up for her, *that he might sanctify her*, having cleansed her by the washing of water with the word, *so that he might present the church to himself in splendor*, without spot or wrinkle or any such thing, *that she might be holy and without blemish*" (Eph. 5:25–27).

The Bible could not be any clearer. The reason for your entire salvation, the design behind your deliverance, the purpose for which God chose you in the first place is holiness.

A NECESSARY GOOD

Not only is holiness the goal of your redemption, it is *necessary* for your redemption. Now before you sound the legalist alarm, tie me up by my own moral bootstraps, and feed my carcass to the Galatians, we should see what Scripture has to say:

- According to Jesus, "Not everyone who says to me, 'Lord, Lord,' will enter the kingdom of heaven, but the one who does the will of my Father who is in heaven" (Matt. 7:21). It's possible to profess the right things and still not be saved. Only those who do the will of the Father will enter the kingdom. And this means hearing Jesus' words and doing them (v. 26).
- Many passages like 1 Corinthians 6:9–10 teach that "the unrighteous will not inherit the kingdom of God." We find this same emphasis in Galatians 5:19–21. It's the consistent and frequent teaching of the Bible that those whose lives are marked by habitual ungodliness will not go to heaven. To find acquittal from God on the last day there must be evidence flowing out of us that grace has flowed into us.
- In particular, 1 John outlines several criteria for determining whether we truly belong to God.[3] Not only will those born of God confess the Son (1 John 2:23; 4:15) and believe that Jesus is the Christ (5:1), they will also keep God's commandments (2:3–4), walk as Christ walked (2:5–6), practice righteousness (2:29), and overcome the world (5:4). "We know that everyone who has been born of God does not keep on sinning, but he who was born of God protects him, and the evil one does not touch him" (5:18).
- Likewise, the book of James makes clear that a faith without accompanying works is no saving faith (James 2:14). "So also faith by itself, if it does not have works, is dead" (v. 17). Many Christians have struggled to reconcile the emphasis on works

---

[3]John Piper finds eleven evidences for the new birth in 1 John. I've included some of them in the following sentence. See *Finally Alive* (Fearn, Ross-shire, UK: Christian Focus, 2009), 125–128.

in James with the emphasis on faith apart from works in Paul. But there is no real conflict. Paul wants us to see that faith is the instrumental means for being right with God. Nothing contributes to our salvation. The only ground is the righteousness of Christ. James, on the other hand, wants us to see that evidences of godliness must accompany true faith. We are justified by faith alone, but the faith that justified us is never alone. Paul is describing true and living faith; James is arguing against a false faith which consists in nothing but spiritually dead intellectual assent (vv. 17, 19, 20, 26).

- And then there's Hebrews 12:14: "Strive for peace with everyone, and for the holiness without which no one will see the Lord." In other words, holiness is not an option. Some of you may be thinking, "Yes, that's absolutely right. We must be holy, and we are counted holy because of Christ." That's true. And in fact, elsewhere in Hebrews we see that holiness—what some theologians call "definitive sanctification"—is a gift we receive through the gospel (10:10, 14). But Hebrews 12 is about the practical outworking of this positional holiness.[4] The holiness of Hebrews 12:14 is not a holiness we receive but a holiness we "strive" for. This makes sense given the context of discipline in the first half of chapter 12. The Hebrews were professing Christians suffering for their Christianity and in danger of making shipwreck of their faith (10:39). So God the Father disciplined them, so that they might be trained by it unto righteousness (12:11). God was intent on making his children holy, because holiness must mark out all those who would have fellowship with a holy God.

There are literally hundreds of verses like these. In 1990 John Piper wrote a long letter everyone should read. It's called "A Letter to a Friend Concerning the So-Called 'Lordship Salvation.'"[5] Back then there was a big debate about whether you could have Christ

---

[4]See Jerry Bridges, *The Pursuit of Holiness* (Colorado Springs: NavPress, 2006), 31–39. Likewise, Peter O'Brien writes, "How then can we pursue what are already God's gifts to us? The proper response is that they should be worked out concretely in our lives as believers" (*The Letter to the Hebrews* [Grand Rapids, MI: Eerdmans, 2010], 472). Later he says, "All believers must press on to the consummation, their perfected holiness, which is indispensable for seeing God" (473).

[5]http://www.desiringgod.org/resource-library/articles/letter-to-a-friend-concerning-the-so-called-lordship-salvation. Accessed June 25, 2011.

as Savior without having him as Lord. John MacArthur wrote *The Gospel According to Jesus* to help people see that the only way to truly follow Jesus is to follow him as Savior *and* Lord.[6] After another minister questioned Piper's support for the book, Piper wrote this "Letter to a Friend." Following the letter itself is an appendix which lists "Texts That Point to the Necessity of Yielding to Christ as Lord in Order to Inherit Eternal Life." It's a long list. Piper mentions six passages that speak to the necessity of doing good for eternal life, thirteen passages on the necessity of obedience, two on the necessity of holiness, two on the need to forgive others, four on the necessity of not living according to the flesh, two on the necessity of being free from the love of money, fourteen on the need to love Christ and God, and six on the necessity of loving others. There are dozens of other verses on the need to love the truth, be childlike, bridle the tongue, persevere, walk in the light, repent, and fight the good fight. In other words, the child of God must be holy.

A NECESSARY EXPLANATION

Let me be clear about something from the very beginning: stressing the necessity of personal holiness should not undermine in any way our confidence in justification by faith alone. The best theologians and the best theological statements have always emphasized the scandalous nature of gospel grace *and* the indispensable need for personal holiness. Faith and good works are both necessary. But one is the root and the other the fruit. God declares us just solely on account of the righteousness of Christ credited (imputed) to us (2 Cor. 5:21). Our innocence in God's sight is in no way grounded in works of love or acts of charity. Whereas a

---

[6]John MacArthur, *The Gospel According to Jesus: What Is Authentic Faith?* (Grand Rapids, MI: Zondervan, 2008).

Catholic might answer the question "What must I do to be saved?" by saying, "Repent, believe, and live in charity,"[7] the apostle Paul answers the same exact question with, "Believe in the Lord Jesus, and you will be saved, you and your household" (Acts 16:31). Getting right with God is entirely and only dependent upon faith.[8]

But there's more we need to say about this faith. The faith that joins you to Christ and makes you right with God is a faith that works itself out in love (Gal. 5:6). On the last day, God will not acquit us because our good works were good enough, but he will look for evidence that our good confession was not phony. It's in this sense that we must be holy.

There is nothing un-Protestant about stressing the need for personal holiness. For example, the Belgic Confession (1561) says, "we do not base our salvation on [good works]." We are justified by faith alone, apart from works. But the Confession also says, "it is impossible for this holy faith to be unfruitful in a human being, seeing that we do not speak of an empty faith but of what Scripture calls 'faith working through love.'"[9] Likewise, the Heidelberg Catechism (1563) teaches that only true faith in Jesus Christ can make us right with God. All we need to do is accept this gift of God with a believing heart. And yet there is no hesitation later on to underline the necessity of holiness: "Can those be saved who do not turn to God from their ungrateful and impenitent ways? By no means. Scripture tells us that no unchaste person, no idolater, no adulterer, no thief, no covetous person, no drunkard, slanderer, robber, or the like is going to inherit the kingdom of God."[10] Statements like these could easily be multiplied by looking

---

[7] Peter J. Kreeft, *Catholic Christianity* (San Francisco: Ignatius, 2001), 130.
[8] This does not mean faith is the good work that saves us. Faith is only the instrumental cause of our salvation. It is the means by which we are joined to Christ and partake in all his benefits (Eph. 1:3; 2:8–9).
[9] Belgic Confession, article 24.
[10] See Heidelberg Catechism, Q/A 60, 61, 87.

at almost any official doctrinal statement that has come out of the Reformation.[11]

In all this it bears repeating that God is the one working in us, giving us the desire and ability to obey. We earn nothing. We are promised everything. But don't be so scared of works-righteousness that you make pale what the Bible writes in bold colors. We are saved by grace through faith (Eph. 2:8). *And* we were created in Christ Jesus for good works (v. 10). Any gospel which purports to save people without also transforming them is inviting easy-believism. If you think being a Christian is nothing more than saying a prayer or joining a church, then you've confused real grace with cheap grace. Those who are justified *will* be sanctified.[12]

There can be no denying or doubting what God has said. It's plain on almost every page of the Bible: we are commanded to be holy, saved to be holy, and, in fact, we must be holy if we are to inherit eternal life.

---

[11]See, for example, The Epitome of the Formula of Concord 4.1 (Lutherans); The Westminster Confession of Faith 13.1 (Presbyterian/Reformed); and Article 13 of Thirty-Nine Articles (Anglican).

[12]In the next chapter I talk about the difference between definitive and progressive sanctification. In one sense those who are justified have already been sanctified (definitively). But it's also right to say that those who are justified will be sanctified (progressively).

Chapter Three

PIETY'S PATTERN

There's no question holiness is one of the central themes in the Bible. The word "holy" occurs more than 600 times in the Bible, more than 700 when you include derivative words like holiness, sanctify, and sanctification. You can't make sense of the Bible without understanding that God is holy and that this holy God is intent on making a holy people to live with him forever in a holy heaven. The whole system of Israel's worship revolves around holiness. That's why you have holy people (the priests), with holy clothes, in a holy land (Canaan), at a holy place (tabernacle/temple), using holy utensils and holy objects, celebrating holy days, living by a holy law, so that they might be a kingdom of priests and a holy nation.

At its most basic, holiness means separation.[1] It is a spatial term. When someone or something is holy it is set apart. In the Gettysburg Address (1863), Abraham Lincoln declared the Civil War battlefield in Pennsylvania to be "hallowed ground." Because of the momentous events that took place in Gettysburg, Cemetery Ridge and Little Round Top would be forever set apart, no longer ordinary or common places, but ones with special significance consecrated for special commemoration. The battlefield at Gettysburg would be holy ground, a place set apart.

In a similar way, God is holy because he is transcendent and

---

[1]David Peterson, *Possessed by God: A New Testament Theology of Sanctification and Holiness* (Downers Grove, IL: InterVarsity Press, 1995), 17.

different from everything he has made. He is separate and distinct, not ordinary or common. He is God, and there is no other (Isa. 45:22). We are called to be holy because God is holy (Lev. 11:44, 45; 19:2; 1 Pet 1:15–16). Our holy God sets us apart to live in a way that reflects, however imperfectly, his holiness.

GOT IT AND STILL GROWING

It's important to realize early in this book—and we'll see this again and again in the chapters ahead—that in one sense we are already holy in Christ. When Christians talk about "sanctification" we usually mean something like "the process of growing in godliness." For centuries theologians have distinguished between justification—the one-time declaration that we are righteous—and sanctification—the ongoing process of becoming righteous. That's a fine way to speak, and it's the way I'll use "sanctification" in these pages. But when the New Testament uses the verb "to sanctify" or the noun "sanctification," it regularly refers to the saving work of God *already* true of us because we belong to Christ.[2] According to Hebrews 10:10, we were sanctified once for all through the offering of the body of Jesus Christ. In Acts 20:32 and 26:18 the "sanctified" ones appears to be a synonym for true Christians. Elsewhere, the "saints" are those who have been "sanctified in Christ Jesus" (1 Cor. 1:2). So Paul can equate being sanctified with being washed and being justified (6:11). When we are joined to Christ by faith, he becomes to us our wisdom, righteousness, sanctification, and redemption (1:30).

In this way of thinking, every Christian is sanctified. We are already set apart, no longer common or profane. Some theologians call this gift of holiness through union with Christ our "definitive

---

[2]Ibid., 27.

sanctification."[3] But this definitive sanctification does not eliminate the need for continuing "progressive sanctification." In Christ
every believer has a once-for-all *positional* holiness, and from
this new identity every Christian is commanded to grow in the
ongoing-for-your-whole-life *process* of holiness (Phil. 2:12–13).
As David Peterson puts it, "Believers are definitively consecrated
to God in order to live dedicated and holy lives, to his glory."[4] In
other words, sanctified is what we are and what we must become.

CHEAP IMITATIONS

But what exactly are we trying to become? God saved us to be
holy—got it. We must be holy as God is holy—check. We are set
apart to serve God—sounds good. But what does holiness actually
look like? Let's try to bring this out of the theological stratosphere
and down to earth where we worship, work, and play. I'll start
with several examples of what holiness is not.

Holiness Is Not Mere Rule Keeping
The word "mere" is critical. Holiness is not less than obeying commands. After all, Jesus didn't say, "If you love me, you will give up
on rules and religion and do whatever makes you feel good." He
said, "If you love me, you will keep my commandments" (John
14:15). So holy people obey, but this is not the same as mere rule
keeping. Godliness is more than basic morality and niceness. The
Pharisees were externally moral, but their hearts were often far
from God (Mark 7:7). Neville Chamberlain was nice when he
appeased Hitler, but Chamberlain is hardly one of history's great
heroes. Don't get me wrong, all things considered I'd rather have
a polite, tree-planting, tax-paying guy who watches PG-13 movies

---

[3]John Murray, "Definitive Sanctification," in *Collected Writings of John Murray*, 4 vols. (Edinburgh: Banner of Truth, 1977), 2:277–284.
[4]Peterson, *Possessed by God*, 27.

move in next door than a heavy-drinking recluse who wagers on cockfighting and dresses like he's late for the Renaissance Fair. But holiness is more than middle-class family values.

It's all too easy to turn the fight of faith into sanctification-by-checklist. Take care of a few bad habits, develop a couple good ones, and you're set. But a moral checklist doesn't take into consideration the idols of the hearts. It may not even have the gospel as part of the equation. And inevitably, checklist spirituality is highly selective. So you end up feeling successful at sanctification because you stayed away from drugs, lost weight, served at the soup kitchen, and renounced Styrofoam. But you've ignored gentleness, humility, joy, and sexual purity. God has not really gotten to your heart. I could probably sell a lot of books if I demanded that Christians read their Bibles two hours a day, throw away their TVs, sell their possessions, adopt three orphans, and move into a commune. We like getting lists. Some of us like getting beat up and then being told exactly what needs to be done to become a true spiritual giant. This sort of exhortation seems promising at first, but it proves ineffective in the long run. Mere rule keeping is not the answer because holiness cannot be reduced to a little ethical refurbishment.

Holiness Is Not Generational Imitation

Because I'm a young person (sort of) writing in a way that challenges young people (among others), it would be tempting for older Christians to assume this book is about how much better things used to be. But as Billy Joel sang (see, I'm not that young!), "the good ol' days weren't always good and tomorrow ain't as bad as it seems." The pursuit of holiness is not the quixotic effort to recreate the 1950s, let alone the 1590s.

Of course, there is much we can learn from previous generations. I often look to the Puritans or the Reformers or my grandparents' generation for theological or ethical examples. But learning from the Puritans does not mean we have to talk like them, dress like them, or abolish Christmas like some of them did. There is no shortcut to sanctification by trying to relive the glory days of some bygone era. "If only things could be like they used to be." Well, that might help with public standards of sexual decency, but the good ol' days weren't so good on race relations. Every generation has both its insights and its blind spots. It takes wisdom to learn from the good and avoid the bad. So yes, I think Christians in general used to be more concerned about personal holiness in certain areas. But does God want us to recreate their world or reintroduce all their strictures about card playing and alcohol prohibition? I doubt it.

Holiness Is Not Generic Spirituality

Has there ever been a phrase more adept at smuggling in doctrinal confusion and moral laxity than the slogan "spiritual, not religious"? Granted, for some people this means, "I want a personal, life-changing relationship with God, not mere church attendance." But more often than not the phrase implies a dislike for theological standards, moral absolutes, and organized religion. Being spiritual in contemporary jargon means you are open to mystery and interested in "spiritual" things like prayer, healing, and inner peace.

True spirituality means being transformed by the Spirit through communion with the Father and the Son. If you are interested in spirituality, your priority should be to grow in the holiness that comes from the Spirit. Righteousness is the goal of Christian discipleship. "In the Christian world today such a statement may sound radical," R. C. Sproul observes. "Many people have spoken to me about being ethical, moral, spiritual, or even pious. But nobody seems to want to talk about being righteous."[5] To be saved by the Spirit's converting grace, sealed by the Spirit's absolute guarantee, and sanctified by the Spirit's indwelling power—that's what it means to be spiritual.

Holiness Is Not "Finding Your True Self"

In secular Western society the truly good person is the one who has learned to be true to himself. For example, Anna Quindlen (who has written for *The New York Times* and *Newsweek*), had this to say to a group of graduating seniors:

> Each of you is as different as your fingertips. Why should you march to any lockstep? Our love of lockstep is our greatest curse, the source of all that bedevils us. It is the source of homophobia, xenophobia, racism, sexism, terrorism, bigotry of every variety and hue, because it tells us that there is one right way to do things, to look, to behave, to feel, when the only right way is to feel your heart hammering inside you and to listen to what its timpani is saying.[6]

It sure feels like Ms. Quindlen is giving my little internal timpani a lot of credit. What if your timpani is homophobic, xenophobic, racist, and sexist? Or can all vice simply be attributed to our love of lockstep—you know, all the bad people follow the crowd and all the good people do their own thing? And what if you follow Quindlen's advice and reject her list of bigotries? Does that make you another lockstep loser? Can you listen to your timpani and the graduation speaker at the same time? I suppose it's the central creed of postmodernism that you can march to the beat of your own drummer as long as it beats in time with mine.

But what if your bongo is out of step with the God of the universe? We've been told there is a good person in all of us. We've

---

[5]R. C. Sproul, *The Holiness of God* (Carol Stream, IL: Tyndale, 1998), 203.
[6]Quoted in *First Things* (August/September, 2002): 95.

been shown in a thousand movies that the purpose of life is to find the real you. We've learned from countless television shows that the highest calling is to believe in yourself. The world most definitely insists on holiness. Don't let anyone tell you it doesn't. But the world's holiness is not found in being true to God; it's found in being true to yourself. And being true to yourself invariably means being true to someone else's definition of tolerance and diversity.

Holiness Is Not the Way of the World

We'll never make progress in holiness if we are waiting for the world to throw us a party for our piety. To be sure, cultural values will sometimes overlap with biblical values. In the West, explicit racism is not tolerated. In Muslim countries, homosexuality is frowned upon. In the Bible Belt, church attendance is encouraged. But the "world" is not another way of saying "the people around us." The world stands for everything that opposes the will of God. In its simplest form, this means "the desires of the flesh and the desires of the eyes and pride of life" (1 John 2:16). Or to put it another way, worldliness is whatever makes sin look normal and righteousness look strange.[7] Some nations and cultures are better than others, but in every society there is a principle of Babylon that makes war against the children of God (Revelation 17–18).

Worldliness is a serious problem. The Bible says that "if anyone loves the world, the love of the Father is not in him" (1 John 2:15). Christians used to talk about worldliness and fear its creeping influence. Today, however, if you talk about dressing in a worldly way or spending your money in a worldly way or seeking worldly entertainment you're bound to hear barely muffled

---

[7]David F. Wells, *God in the Wasteland: The Reality of Truth in a World of Fading Dreams* (Grand Rapids, MI: Eerdmans, 1994), 29.

laughter. Worldliness is what our grandparents were uptight about. We have a planet to save and no time to concern ourselves with such trivialities. We simply don't believe that friendship with the world is enmity with God (James 4:4).

Many Christians have the mistaken notion that if only we were better Christians, everyone would appreciate us. They don't realize that holiness comes with a cost. Sure, you can focus on the virtues the world likes. But if you pursue true religion that cares for orphans *and* promotes purity (James 1:27), you'll lose some of the friends you were so desperate to make. Becoming a living sacrifice, holy and acceptable to God, requires you to resist the world which wants to press you into its mold (Rom. 12:1–2). Saving yourself for marriage, staying sober on Friday night, turning down a promotion to stay at your church, refusing to say the f-word, turning off the television—these are the kinds of things the world doesn't understand. Don't expect them to. The world provides no cheerleaders on the pathway to godliness.

THE REAL DEAL

We've seen five examples of what holiness isn't. Now let's go to the positive side and see what holiness actually looks like.

Holiness Looks Like the Renewal of God's Image in Us

Adam and Eve were created in God's image, after his likeness (Gen. 1:26). But in Adam's sin, the human race was given over to corruption (Rom. 5:12–21). We are still image-bearers (Gen. 9:6; James 3:9), but the image has been distorted (Gen. 6:5; Eccles. 7:29). The goal of sanctification is the renewal of this image. The holy person is being renewed in knowledge after the image of the Creator (Col. 3:10), which means growing in righteousness and holiness (Eph. 4:24). This does not happen all at once, but rather, we are transformed into the image of God from one degree of glory to another (2 Cor. 3:18). God is holy, so most basically being holy means being like God. This is why it's so critical that Christians know the character and work of the one they worship. If you want to know what holiness looks like, look at God.

Holiness Looks Like a Life Marked by Virtue Instead of Vice

But what does God-like character look like in God's people? One way to answer that question is to look at every command and example in the Bible. But a quicker approach is to examine the lists of vices and virtues in the New Testament. These provide a useful summary of wickedness and holiness.

Here are the sort of vices that characterize the wicked and the sort of people who will not enter the kingdom:

- Mark 7:21–22: evil thoughts, sexual immorality, theft, murder, adultery, coveting, wickedness, deceit, sensuality, envy, slander, pride, foolishness.
- Romans 1:24–31: impurity, homosexual relations, all manner of unrighteousness, evil, covetousness, malice, envy, murder, strife, deceit, maliciousness, gossip, slander, hatred of God, disobedient to parents, foolish, faithless, heartless, ruthless.
- Romans 13:13: orgies, drunkenness, sexual immorality, sensuality, quarreling, jealousy.
- 1 Corinthians 6:9–10: sexual immorality, idolatry, adultery, men who practice homosexuality, thieves, the greedy, drunkards, revilers, swindlers.
- Galatians 5:19–21: sexual immorality, impurity, sensuality, idolatry, sorcery, enmity, strife, jealousy, fits of anger, rivalries, dissensions, divisions, envy, drunkenness, orgies and things like these.
- Colossians 3:5–9: sexual immorality, impurity, passion, evil desire, covetousness (which is idolatry), anger, wrath, malice, slander, obscene talk, lying.
- 1 Timothy 1:9–10: unholy, profane, those who strike their fathers and mothers, murderers, the sexually immoral, men who prac-

tice homosexuality, enslavers, liars, perjurers, and whatever else is contrary to sound doctrine.

- Revelation 21:8: the cowardly, the faithless, the detestable, murderers, the sexually immoral, sorcerers, idolaters, and all liars.

On the flip side, here are the sorts of virtues found in God's people:

- Romans 12:9–21: genuine love, hatred for evil, steadfastness in what is good, brotherly affection, excelling in showing honor, zealous, fervent in spirit, serving the Lord, joyful in hope, patient in tribulation, constant in prayer, generous, hospitable, blessing enemies, rejoicing with those who rejoice and weeping with those who weep, harmonious, humble not haughty, associating with the lowly, honorable, peaceable, does not repay evil for evil, overcomes evil with good.
- 1 Corinthians 13:4–7: loving, patient, kind, not envious, not boastful, nor arrogant, not rude, not selfish, not irritable, not resentful, no joy in wrongdoing, rejoices with the truth, bears all things, believes all things, hopes all things, endures all things.
- Galatians 5:22–23: love, joy, peace, patience, kindness, goodness, faithfulness, gentleness, self-control.
- Colossians 3:12–15: compassionate hearts, kindness, humility, meekness, patience, bearing with one another, forgiving one another, love, peace, gratitude.
- 2 Peter 1:5–7: virtue, knowledge, self-control, steadfastness, godliness, brotherly affection, and love.

As you can see, there is a good deal of overlap and a number of common themes that provide a pretty clear picture of what godliness looks like. We don't have specifics on how long to pray each day or how much money to give to the poor. Christians often equate holiness with activism and spiritual disciplines. And while it's true that activism is often the outgrowth of holiness and spiritual disciplines are necessary for the cultivation of holiness, the pattern of piety in the Scripture is more explicitly about our character. We put off sin and put on righteousness. We put to death the deeds of the flesh and put on Christ. To use the older language, we pursue the mortification of the old man and the vivification of the new.

You can think of holiness, to employ a metaphor, as the sanctification of your body. The mind is filled with the knowledge of God and fixed on what is good. The eyes turn away from sensuality and shudder at the sight of evil. The mouth tells the truth and refuses to gossip, slander, or speak what is coarse or obscene. The spirit is earnest, steadfast, and gentle. The heart is full of joy instead of hopelessness, patience instead of irritability, kindness instead of anger, humility instead of pride, and thankfulness instead of envy. The sexual organs are pure, being reserved for the privacy of marriage between one man and one woman. The feet move toward the lowly and away from senseless conflict, divisions, and wild parties. The hands are quick to help those in need and ready to fold in prayer. This is the anatomy of holiness.

Holiness Looks Like a Clean Conscience

We don't think about the conscience as much as we should. But the Bible has more to say about the "little voice in your head" than you might think. One of the great blessings of justification is a clean conscience before God. The accusations of the Devil can be silenced by the blood of the Lamb (Rev. 12:10–11; cf. Rom. 8:1; Zech. 3:2). But even after we've been reconciled to God, we must pay attention to our consciences. According to Romans 2:15, we all have the law written on our hearts so that our consciences can either accuse or excuse us. God speaks to us through the conscience, and when we ignore that voice we put ourselves in grave danger.

Of course, the conscience is not infallible. We can have an evil conscience that doesn't turn away from sin (Heb. 10:22). We can have a seared conscience that no longer feels bad for evil (1 Tim. 4:2). We can have a weak conscience that feels bad for things that aren't really bad (1 Cor. 8:7–12). And we can have a defiled conscience that loses its ability to discern right from wrong (Titus 1:15).[8] The conscience is no substitute for the Bible and must never be in opposition to it. But a good conscience is a gift from God. As we pursue holiness we must always be mindful of God's voice speaking to us through a tender conscience informed by the Word of God. It will lead us not into temptation and will deliver us from evil.

It's critical that the Christian's conscience be clean. That's why Paul said, "I always take pains to have a clear conscience toward both God and man" (Acts 24:16). He often mentioned the testimony of his conscience as his "boast" and as an indication of his moral uprightness (Rom. 9:1; 2 Cor. 1:12; 4:2). Paul recognized he could be wrong in his self-assessment, but it was important to him not to be aware of anything against himself (1 Cor. 4:4). When we violate our sense of right and wrong, even if the action in itself is not sinful, we are guilty of sin. "Whatever does not proceed from faith is sin" (Rom. 14:23). That means, if you don't believe what you are doing is acceptable, then it's not acceptable for you to do it. You must not ignore your conscience.

Suppose you grew up thinking alcohol was wrong. I mean, always wrong, like, you'd rather drink Drano than Bud Light. But now you are at a church that says alcohol is not sinful, so long as you are of legal age and don't drink to excess. What should you do? If you are convinced that the Bible approves of alcohol in moderation, then you are free to drink (1 Tim. 5:23; cf. John 2:1–11).[9]

---

[8] See Jerry White, *Honesty, Morality, and Conscience* (Colorado Springs: NavPress, 1996), 35–41.
[9] Although I affirm that Christians can drink alcohol, I don't personally. In small measure, I probably never gave alcohol much of a chance because I have a weak conscience. But mainly, it doesn't smell good, look good, or taste good to me. Ask my friends and they'll tell you I feel this way about many things normal people consume. I have what you might call "a sensitive palate."

But if it still feels dirty to you, you should abstain. Even if the Bible gives the green light, the red light in your conscience should not be transgressed. This is why passages like 1 Corinthians 8 and 10 and Romans 14 rebuke "strong conscience" Christians who lead "weak conscience" Christians to do things that feel wrong to them. The danger is that, if you violate your conscience in this matter (even though the action is not forbidden), you'll learn to disobey your conscience in other matters.

Let me give you two examples from my own life where I have tried (and sometimes have failed) to listen to my conscience. The first has to do with movies, and the second with dating.

I'm not a big movie buff. I've seen my fair share, but if I have an evening free I'd rather read a book, play a game, or watch sports than take in a movie. My wife, on the other hand, likes movies, mostly BBC costume dramas and other pretty innocent fare. But sometimes there will be scenes that unsettle me. Usually these are sexual or sensual in some way. It doesn't take much skin for me to feel guilty. Is this because as a guy I am more susceptible to visual temptation? Definitely that's part of it. Is my sensitive conscience a sign that I am progressing in sanctification? I'm not sure. I have to be careful (with movies in particular) that I don't assume my pangs of conscience mean everyone else tuned in is committing sin. But when my conscience is pricked I should not continue watching. A tender conscience is a terrible thing to waste.

Incidentally, I've learned over the years that the simplest way to judge gray areas like movies, television, and music is to ask one simple question: can I thank God for this?[10] (We are to give thanks

---

[10]Compare 1 Corinthians 10:23–33. Jerry Bridges suggests four questions for discerning matters of Christian liberty: Is it helpful? Does it bring me under its power? Does it hurt others? Does it glorify God? (*The Pursuit of Holiness* [Colorado Springs: NavPress, 2006], 88). See also 1 Timothy 4:4–5, "For everything created by God is good, and nothing is to be rejected if it is received with thanksgiving, for it is made holy by the word of God and prayer."

in all circumstances, right?) Not too long ago my wife and I went to the movie theater to watch one of the summer blockbusters. It was a fun PG-13 movie, and you'd probably say it didn't really have any bad parts. But it was very sensual and suggestive in several places. I got done with the movie (yes, I watched the whole thing) and thought, "Can I really thank God for this?" Now, I'm not a total kill-joy. I like to laugh and enjoy life. I can thank God for the Chicago Bears, Hot N' Readys, and Brian Regan. But I wonder if after most of our entertainment we could sincerely get down on our knees and say, "Thank you, God, for this good gift." Something to think about.

The other example concerns dating. When my wife and I were dating we struggled with boundaries in our physical relationship. As is the case for many couples (even Christian ones, and even those training for pastoral ministry), the struggle only intensified after we got engaged. I sought advice from several Christians I respected, some married and some engaged like me. They gave conflicting advice on "how far was too far." Obviously, sex was out of the question, and so were a lot of other things on the way to sex. But where should Christians draw the line? What I know now is that even though we stopped far short of sex, I did not lead well in our physical relationship. If nothing else, my wife and I sinned against our consciences, no matter if some of my friends could "go farther" and walk away guilt-free. It was only after we were married that we saw clearly our sin and I was able to ask my wife and the Lord for forgiveness.

When it comes to levels of physical intimacy before marriage, I believe many Christians are objectively sinning, whether they feel like they are or not. But I'll say more on that later. What I want you to see at the moment is that questionable choices, or even acceptable ones, are sinful for you when they don't feel right. Christians should not violate, nor pressure others to violate, what their consciences tell them is wrong.

Holiness Looks Like Obedience to God's Commands

It sounds really spiritual to say God is interested in a relationship, not in rules. But it's not biblical. From top to bottom the Bible is full of commands. They aren't meant to stifle a relationship with God, but to protect it, seal it, and define it. Never forget: first God delivered the Israelites from Egypt, *then* he gave them the law. God's people were not redeemed *by* observing the law, but they were redeemed *so they might obey* the law. "By this we know that we have come to know him, if we keep his commandments" (1 John 2:3). We can talk all day long about our love for God, but if we do not keep his commandments we are liars and the truth is not in us (v. 4). If we love Jesus, we'll obey his Word (John 14:23). Just like, if you love your wife, you'll keep your vow to be faithful to her as long as you both shall live. The demand for sexual fidelity does not pervert the marriage relationship; it promotes and demonstrates it. In the same way, God's commands are given as a means of grace so that we might grow in godliness and show that we love him.

The rule for holiness is the law, in particular the Ten Commandments. Christians don't always agree on how to view the law (something I'll say more about in the next chapter), but historically the church has put the Ten Commandments at the center of its instruction for God's people, especially for children and new believers. For centuries discipleship instruction (catechesis) has been based on three things: the Apostles' Creed, the Lord's Prayer, and the Ten Commandments. If you wanted the basics of the Christian faith, you learned these three things. And if you wanted to know how to live a holy life, you followed the law of God summarized in the Ten Commandments.

You may think of the Ten Commandments as a painful memorization exercise for five-year-olds, but the "Ten Words" (or Decalogue) from Exodus 20 are central to the ethics of the New Testament. For Jesus and the apostles, the Ten Commandments provided a basic summary of God's ethical intentions for everyone everywhere.[11] When a rich young man asked Jesus what he must do to inherit eternal life, Jesus replied, "You know the commandments," and he listed the commands in the so-called second table of the law (Mark 10:19). The only "horizontal" command he didn't mention was "do not covet." And that's because he wanted to expose the rich man's greed. True, Jesus used the law in this instance for its convicting power more than anything else, but it still shows the place the Ten Commandments held as a summary of God's will (cf. 1 Tim. 1:8–11).

We see the same thing in Romans 13:9, where Paul rattles off four of the commandments and makes reference to "any other commandment." What's amazing is that Paul says in verse 8, "Owe no one anything, except to love each other, for the one who loves another has fulfilled the law." Then he moves on to the Ten Commandments. Obeying the commandments is how we fulfill the law of love, and love is at the heart of holiness (v. 10). If you care about love you will love to obey the Ten Commandments.

Holiness Looks Like Christlikeness

If holiness looks like the restoration of the image of God in us, then it shouldn't be surprising that holiness also looks like

---

[11]Even among Christians who affirm the importance of the Ten Commandments, there is disagreement on the abiding significance of the Sabbath command. It's beyond the scope of this book to wade into this discussion. All I want to point out is that even if literal Sabbath observance has been abolished, this doesn't mean we are free to disobey the fourth commandment. What it means is that the fourth commandment has been transformed by Christ. So now we obey the Sabbath commandment, not by resting on Saturday but by resting in Christ (apart from works) for our salvation (Heb. 4:9–10). See Christopher John Donato, ed., *Perspectives on the Sabbath: Four Views* (Nashville: B&H Academic, 2011).

Christlikeness, for Jesus Christ is the image of the invisible God (Col. 1:15) and the exact imprint of his nature (Heb. 1:3). The whole goal of our salvation is that we should be conformed to the image of God's Son (Rom. 8:29).

We see in Jesus the best, most practical, most human example of what it means to be holy. He is our model for love (John 13:34), our model for humility (Phil. 2:5–8), our model for facing temptation (Heb. 4:15), our model for steadfastness in the midst of suffering (1 Pet. 4:1–2), and our model for obedience to the Father (John 6:38; 14:31). We see all the virtues of holiness perfectly aligned in Christ. He was always gentle, but never soft. He was bold, but never brash. He was pure, but never prudish. He was full of mercy but not at the expense of justice. He was full of truth but not at the expense of grace. In everything he was submissive to his heavenly Father, and he gave everything for his sheep. He obeyed his parents, kept the law of God, and forgave his enemies. He never lusted, never coveted, and never lied. In all that Jesus Christ did, during his whole life and especially as his life came to an end, he loved God with his whole being and loved his neighbor as himself.

If somewhere down the road you forget the Ten Commandments or can't recall the fruit of the Spirit or don't seem to remember any particular attributes of God, you can still remember what holiness is by simply remembering his name.

Chapter Four

THE IMPETUS FOR
THE IMPERATIVES

Many moons ago, when I was a little more svelte and the fast-twitch muscles twitched a little bit faster, I ran cross-country and track. I was either so good or so bad that I tried every event in track at least once. I especially liked distance running. Today, long-distance means running for thirty minutes straight and trying not to empty my inhaler in the process, but back in high school and college I could run for eight or ten or twelve miles and talk the whole way.

One of the things we talked about, I must confess, is how we might trim the day's workout just a wee bit. I was of the Malachi school of running—no harm in cutting a few corners (Mal. 1:6–8, 13). I specialized in straight lines through rounded parking lots. Some of my friends, however, adhered to the Martin Luther "sin boldly" theory of shortcuts. One time they chopped a long run almost in half by cutting through a couple of muck fields. It seemed like a good idea at the time: eliminate the middle portion of the route by taking a left at the celery farm. But unfortunately there are two problems with running through muck. One, the muck sticks to your legs, making your shortcut rather obvious. And two, it's almost impossible to run on muck. In the end, the shortcut proved to be quite a long cut and my friends had nothing to show for their crime except dirty shoes.

It's true in life, as it's true in running around muck fields, that the right way to go is also the best way to go. When God gives us commands, he means to help us run the race to completion, not to slow us down. In his *Reflections on the Psalms*, C. S. Lewis pondered how anyone could "delight" in the law of the Lord. Respect, maybe. Assent, perhaps. But how could anyone find the law so exhilarating? And yet, the more he thought about it, the more Lewis came to understand how the psalmist's delight made sense. "Their delight in the Law," Lewis observed, "is a delight in having touched firmness; like the pedestrian's delight in feeling the hard road beneath his feet after a false short cut has long entangled him in muddy fields."[1] The law is good because firmness is good. God cares enough to show us his ways and direct our paths. How awful it would be to inhabit this world, have some idea that there is a God, and yet not know what he desires from us.[2] Divine statutes are a gift to us. God gives us law because he loves.

WHAT'S LEFT FOR THE LAW?

Of all the thorny theological issues in the Bible, the most difficult, in my opinion, is the role of the law in the life of the Christian. On the one hand, the Christian is no longer under the law, but under grace (Rom. 6:14; 7:6). The law of Moses was only a temporary tutor, leading us to Christ (Gal. 3:23–26). On the other hand, we know the law is holy, righteous, and good (Rom. 7:12) and that God still expects us to obey his "perfect" and "royal" law (James 1:25; 2:8). The same Paul who says we are not "under the law" (1 Cor. 9:20) also says he is "under the law of Christ" (v. 21). Christians often speak of the three uses of the law. The first is to lead us to Christ by convicting us of sin. The second is

[1] C. S. Lewis, *Reflections on the Psalms* (New York: Harcourt Brace Jovanovich, 1958), 62.
[2] This line comes from my friend and PCA pastor Jason Helopolous.

to restrain wickedness in the world. The third use is to help us learn the nature of the Lord's will, acting as a kind of blueprint for holiness. Christians generally agree with the first two points. The controversy is whether the so-called third use is a legitimate, or even primary, purpose of the law.

I'm the pastor at University *Reformed* Church, which means I support the third use of the law, seeing as how this Calvinist understanding of the law is enshrined in every Reformed confession and catechism. But you don't have to belong to a confessional Reformed church to believe in the importance of the law in the believer's life. Some Christians think the law continues to be God's tool for the promotion of holiness. Other Christians think the law no longer has direct application for New Testament believers. These two sides are not always that far apart. Those who affirm the ongoing importance of the law usually distinguish between the parts of the law that are directly applicable and the parts that can be applied only indirectly. Typically, this has meant that the moral law (e.g., the Ten Commandments) is directly normative, but the civil and judicial aspects of the law *point* to what is true for all people at all times.[3] On the other hand, those who argue that we are not obligated to keep the law are usually quick to clarify that they still think the law contains universally true moral principles.[4] Both sides recognize that the law was given in a certain context at a particular moment in redemptive history. And both sides

---

[3] See Westminster Confession 19:2–4, which uses the phrase "general equity" to describe what I call "pointing." Similarly, Calvin says "the whole cultus of the law, taken literally and not as shadows and figures corresponding to the truth, will be utterly ridiculous" (*Institutes* 2.7.1).

[4] See Thomas R. Schreiner, *40 Questions about Christians and Biblical Law* (Grand Rapids, MI: Kregel, 2010), 99: "Strictly speaking, the idea that believers are under the third use of the law is mistaken, for we have seen that the entire [Mosaic] law is abolished for believers. Still, the notion is not entirely wrong since Paul's teaching is filled with exhortations that call upon believers to live in a way that pleases God. . . . Even though the Old Testament law is not literally binding upon believers, we see principles and patterns and moral norms that still apply to us today since the Old Testament is the word of God." See also Douglas J. Moo, *The Epistle to the Romans* (Grand Rapids, MI: Eerdmans, 1996), 415–416.

recognize that the law still has something to say about how we live as Christians.[5]

Part of the confusion in all this is that "law" means different things in the Bible. It can refer to the Old Testament Scriptures, the Torah (i.e., the first five books of the Bible), the Mosaic law, or simply what God requires his people to do.[6] So while we are not "under the law" in the sense that we are condemned by the law or bound to the Old Covenant of Moses (2 Cor. 3:6; Heb. 8:13), we are "under law" in so far as we are still obligated to obey our Lord and every expression of his will for our lives (1 Cor. 9:21). The law of God cannot save—that's legalism. But everything in the Bible is for our edification, that we may be equipped for good works (2 Tim. 3:16–17). So whatever the Bible teaches, we should believe. And whatever it commands—by precept, example, story, or song—we should do.[7]

THE GRACE OF LAW

That last sentence—we should do what the Bible tells us to do— is obvious to most Christians. But I want to go a step further. I want you to unashamedly love, and not be afraid to land on, the imperatives of Scripture. I know the danger with imperatives is that we end up getting all law and no gospel, making Christianity a religion of good advice instead of good news. If the law is what convicts and condemns and the gospel is what gives grace and forgives, then the only good thing about law is that it can lead us to gospel. But let's be careful. There is nothing sub-Christian in talking about obedience to God's commands. There is nothing

---

[5]See, for example, Willem VanGemeren's response to Douglas Moo in *Five Views on Law and Gospel* (Grand Rapids, MI: Zondervan, 1999), 378–379.

[6]Schreiner, *40 Questions*, 19–23.

[7]See John M. Frame, *The Doctrine of the Christian Life* (Phillipsburg, NJ: P&R, 2008), 178. Of course, to understand what the Bible commands for us today we need to pay attention to the flow of redemptive history, cultural context, and the difference between description and prescription.

inherently anti-gospel in being exhorted to keep the imperatives of Scripture. There is nothing ungracious about divine demands. Just the opposite, in fact—there is grace in getting law.

We usually think of law leading us to gospel. And this is true—we see God's standards, see our sin, and then see our need for a Savior. But it's just as true that gospel leads to law. In Exodus, first God delivered his people from Egypt, then he gave the Ten Commandments. In Romans, Paul expounds on the sovereign free grace and the atoning work of Christ in chapters 1–11, and then in chapters 12–16 he shows us how to live in light of these mercies. In John 4, Christ tells the Samaritan woman about the living water welling up to eternal life, and then he exposes her sin and instructs her to worship God in spirit and truth. I'm not suggesting any kind of rigid evangelistic formula. I simply want to show that the good news of the gospel leads to gracious instructions for obeying God.

THE LAW OF LOVE AND THE LOVE OF LAW

Some Christians make the mistake of pitting love against law, as if the two were mutually exclusive. You either have a religion of love or a religion of law. But such an equation is profoundly unbiblical. For starters, "love" is a command of the law (Deut. 6:5; Lev. 19:18; Matt. 22:36–40). If you enjoin people to love, you are giving them law. Conversely, if you tell them law doesn't matter, then neither does love, which is the summary of the law.

Furthermore, consider the close connection Jesus makes between love and law. We've already seen that for Jesus there is no love for him apart from keeping the law (John 14:15). But he says even more than this. Jesus connects communion with God with keeping commandments. When we keep Christ's commandments, we love him. And when we love Christ, the Father loves us.

And whomever the Father loves, Christ loves and reveals himself to them (John 14:21). So, there is no abiding in Christ's love apart from keeping Christ's commandments (John 15:10). Which means there is no fullness of joy apart from the pursuit of holiness (v. 11).

God's law is an expression of his grace because it is also an expression of his character. Commands show us what God is like, what he prizes, what he detests, what it means to be holy as God is holy. To hate all rules is to hate God himself who ordained his rules to reflect his nature. The law is God's plan for his sanctified people to enjoy communion with him. That's why the Psalms are full of declarations of delight regarding God's commands. Even with the passing of the Mosaic covenant, surely the psalms set an example for us. The happy man delights in the law of the Lord and meditates on it day and night (Ps. 1:2). The precepts and rules of the Lord are sweeter than honey and more to be desired than gold (Ps. 19:10). Yes, the law can incite the natural man to sin (Rom. 7:7–11). But God's people rejoice in his statutes and behold wondrous things out of his law (Ps. 119:18). They long to be steadfast in keeping his statutes (v. 5). In the eyes of the believer, the law is still true and good; it is our hope, our comfort, and our song.

Let's not be afraid to land on law—never as the means of meriting justification, but as the proper expression of having received it. It's not wrong for a sermon to conclude with something we have to do. It's not inappropriate that our counseling exhort one another to obedience. Legalism is a problem in the church, but so is antinomianism. Granted, I don't hear anyone saying, "let's continue in sin that grace may abound" (see Rom. 6:1). That's the worst form of antinomianism. But strictly speaking, antinomianism simply means no-law, and some Christians have very little place for the law in their pursuit of holiness. One scholar says, about an antinomian pastor from seventeenth-century England, "He believed that the law served a useful purpose in convincing men of their need of a Saviour; nevertheless, he gave it little or no place in the life of a Christian since he held that 'free grace is the teacher of good works.'"[8] Emphasizing free grace is not the problem. The problem is in assuming that good works will invariably flow from nothing but a diligent emphasis on the gospel. Many Christians, including preachers, don't know what to do with commands and are afraid to talk directly about obedience. The world may think we're homophobic, but *nomophobia* (fear of law) may be our bigger problem.

The irony is that if we make every imperative into a command to believe the gospel more fully, we turn the gospel into one more thing we have to get right, and faith becomes the one thing we need to be better at. If only we *really* believed, obedience would take care of itself. No need for commands or effort. But the Bible does not reason this way. It has no problem with the word "therefore." Grace, grace, grace, *therefore*, stop doing this, start doing that, and obey the commands of God. Good works should always be rooted in the good news of Christ's death and resurrection, but I believe we are expecting too much from the "flow" and not doing enough to teach that obedience to the law—from a willing spirit, as made possible by the Holy Spirit—is the proper response to free grace.

For as much as Luther derided the misuse of the law, he did not reject the positive role of the law in the believer's life. The Lutheran Formula of Concord is absolutely right when it says, "We believe, teach, and confess that the preaching of the Law is to be urged with diligence, not only upon the unbelieving and impenitent, but also upon true believers, who are truly converted, regenerate, and justified by faith" (Epitome 6.2). Preachers must preach the law without embarrassment. Parents must insist on obedience without

---

[8]Peter Toon, *The Emergence of Hyper-Calvinism in English Nonconformity 1689–1765* (Eugene, OR: Wipf & Stock, 1967), 54. The line is in reference to Tobias Crisp (1600–1643).

shame. The law can, and should, be urged upon true believers—not to condemn, but to correct and to promote Christlikeness. Both the indicatives of Scripture and the imperatives are from God, for our good, and given in grace.

THE MEDICINE FOR OUR MOTIVATION

One of the reasons why I think Christians get tired of hearing about the law is because they never hear *why* they should obey the law. The imperatives hit us like a ton of study Bibles because we aren't given any motivation for keeping God's commands. Everything boils down to, "God said it, so do it." Or on the opposite end of the spectrum, some Christians make it sound like gratitude is the only legitimate motivation for obedience: "Look at everything Christ has done for you. Now be thankful and let the good works flow." These are both true motivations for holiness, but they aren't the only ones.[9]

Jesus is the Great Physician, and like any good doctor he writes different prescriptions for different illnesses. The gospel is always the remedy for the guilt of sin, but when it comes to overcoming the presence of sin, Jesus has many doses at his disposal. He knows that personalities and sins and situations all vary. So what might be good motivation for holiness in a certain situation with a particular person facing a specific sin may not be the best prescription for someone else in different circumstances. Jesus has many medicines for our motivation. He is not like a high school athletic trainer who tells everyone to "ice it and take a couple ibuprofen." He's not some quack doctor who always prescribes bloodletting. "High cholesterol? Here's a leach. Overactive bladder? I got a leach for that. Gout? A couple leaches will take the

---

[9]I'll say more about this topic in chapter 6, in particular, how God uses the gospel and his promises to empower our pursuit of holiness.

edge off." The good news is that the Bible is a big, diverse, wise book, and in it you can find a variety of prescriptions to encourage obedience to God's commands.[10]

Here are just some of the ways in which the Bible motivates us to pursue holiness:

- *Duty*. "The end of the matter; all has been heard. Fear God and keep his commandments, for this is the whole duty of man" (Eccles. 12:13).
- *God knows all and sees all*. "For God will bring every deed into judgment, with every secret thing, whether good or evil" (Eccles. 12:14).
- *It's right*. "Children, obey your parents in the Lord, for this is right" (Eph. 6:1).
- *It's for our good*. "Be careful to obey all these words that I command you, that it may go well with you and with your children after you forever, when you do what is good and right in the sight of the LORD your God." (Deut. 12:28).
- *God's example*. "Be kind to one another, tenderhearted, forgiving one another, as God in Christ forgave you" (Eph. 4:32).
- *Christ's example*. "And walk in love, as Christ loved us and gave himself up for us, a fragrant offering and sacrifice to God" (Eph. 5:2).
- *Assurance*. "Therefore, brothers, be all the more diligent to confirm your calling and election, for if you practice these qualities you will never fall" (2 Pet. 1:10).

---

[10]For example, the Heidelberg Catechism gives four reasons for doing good: to show we are thankful for what God has done, so he may be praised through us, so we may be assured of our faith by its fruits, and so that by our godly living our neighbors may be won over to Christ (Q/A 86). Likewise, John Owen mentions several gospel grounds for our obedience: good works are necessary because God has appointed them; our holiness is one special end of God's love which is meant to redound to God's glory; our obedience brings God glory and honor; it brings us honor and peace and makes us useful to God; it benefits the world by convicting sinners, converting others, benefiting society; it testifies that we are justified and is a pledge of our adoption; it is a means of our thankfulness (*Communion with the Triune God*, ed. Kelly M. Kapic and Justin Taylor [Wheaton, IL: Crossway, 2007], 303–309). Francis Turretin lists five "principal motives to sanctification," all of which can be derived from Christ's death: the foulness of sin, God's hatred of sin, the unspeakable love of Christ, the right Christ has over us, and "that being dead to sin we should live unto righteousness" (*Institutes of Elenctic Theology*, trans. George Musgrave Giger, ed. James T. Dennison, Jr., 3 vols. [Phillipsburg, NJ: P&R, 1994], 2:692).

- *Being effective as a Christian.* "For if these qualities are yours and are increasing, they keep you from being ineffective or unfruitful in the knowledge of our Lord Jesus Christ" (2 Pet. 1:8).
- *Jesus' return.* "Since all these things are thus to be dissolved, what sort of people ought you to be in lives of holiness and godliness, waiting for and hastening the coming of the day of God, because of which the heavens will be set on fire and dissolved, and the heavenly bodies will melt as they burn!" (2 Pet. 3:11–12).
- *The world is not our home.* "Beloved, I urge you as sojourners and exiles to abstain from the passions of the flesh, which wage war against your soul" (1 Pet. 2:11).
- *To win over our neighbors.* "Keep your conduct among the Gentiles honorable, so that when they speak against you as evildoers, they may see your good deeds and glorify God on the day of visitation" (1 Pet. 2:12).
- *To lift up a nation.* "Righteousness exalts a nation, but sin is a reproach to any people" (Prov. 14:34).
- *For the public good.* "You are the salt of the earth, but if salt has lost its taste, how shall its saltiness be restored?" (Matt. 5:13a).
- *For the sake of our prayers.* "Likewise, husbands, live with your wives in an understanding way, showing honor to the woman as the weaker vessel, since they are heirs with you of the grace of life, so that your prayers may not be hindered" (1 Pet. 3:7).
- *The futility of sin.* "And which of you by being anxious can add a single hour to his span of life?" (Matt. 6:27).
- *The folly of sin.* "And everyone who hears these words of mine and does not do them will be like a foolish man who built his house on the sand. And the rain fell, and the floods came, and the winds blew and beat against that house, and it fell, and great was the fall of it" (Matt. 7:26–27).
- *The promise of future grace.* "But seek first the kingdom of God and his righteousness, and all these things will be added to you" (Matt. 6:33).
- *The promise of future judgment.* "Beloved, never avenge yourselves, but leave it to the wrath of God, for it is written, 'Vengeance is mine, I will repay, says the Lord'" (Rom. 12:19).
- *The fear of future judgment.* "For if we go on sinning deliberately after receiving the knowledge of the truth, there no longer

remains a sacrifice for sins, but a fearful expectation of judgment, and a fury of fire that will consume the adversaries" (Heb. 10:26–27).

- *The surety of our inheritance.* "For you had compassion on those in prison, and you joyfully accepted the plundering of your property, since you knew that you yourselves had a better possession and an abiding one" (Heb. 10:34).

- *The communion of the saints.* "Therefore, since we are surrounded by so great a cloud of witnesses, let us also lay aside every weight, and sin which clings so closely, and let us run with endurance the race that is set before us" (Heb. 12:1).

- *The good examples of others.* "Remember your leaders, those who spoke to you the word of God. Consider the outcome of their way of life, and imitate their faith" (Heb. 13:7).

- *The bad examples of others.* "Now these things took place as examples for us, that we might not desire evil as they did" (1 Cor. 10:6).

- *We were created for good works.* "For we are his workmanship, created in Christ Jesus for good works, which God prepared beforehand, that we should walk in them" (Eph. 2:10).

- *God is the master and we are his servants.* "So you also, when you have done all that you were commanded, say, 'We are unworthy servants; we have only done what was our duty'" (Luke 17:10).

- *The fear of the Lord.* "Therefore, knowing the fear of the Lord, we persuade others" (2 Cor. 5:11a).

- *The love of the Lord.* "Beloved, if God so loved us, we also ought to love one another" (1 John 4:11).

- *To make God manifest.* "No one has ever seen God; if we love one another, God abides in us and his love is perfected in us" (1 John 4:12).

- *In gratitude for grace.* "I appeal to you therefore, brothers, by the mercies of God, to present your bodies as a living sacrifice, holy and acceptable to God, which is your spiritual worship" (Rom. 12:1).

- *For the glory of God.* "Or do you not know that your body is a temple of the Holy Spirit within you, whom you have from God? You are not your own, for you were bought with a price. So glorify God in your body" (1 Cor. 6:19–20).

- *The character of God.* "For I am the LORD your God. Consecrate yourselves therefore, and be holy, for I am holy" (Lev. 11:44a).
- *The work of God.* "I am the LORD your God, who brought you out of the land of Egypt, out of the house of slavery. You shall have no other gods before me" (Ex. 20:2–3).
- *To please God.* "Do not neglect to do good and to share what you have, for such sacrifices are pleasing to God" (Heb. 13:16).
- *To avoid the devil's snares.* "Be angry and do not sin; do not let the sun go down on your anger, and give no opportunity to the devil" (Eph. 4:26–27).
- *For an eternal reward.* "They are to do good, to be rich in good works, to be generous and ready to share, thus storing up treasure for themselves as a good foundation for the future, so that they may take hold of that which is truly life" (1 Tim. 6:18–19).
- *Because Christ has all authority.* "All authority in heaven and on earth has been given to me. Go therefore and make disciples of all nations, baptizing them in the name of the Father and of the Son and of the Holy Spirit, teaching them to observe all that I have commanded you" (Matt. 28:18b–20a).
- *Love for Christ.* "If you love me, you will keep my commandments" (John 14:15).
- *Fullness of joy.* "If you keep my commandments, you will abide in my love, just as I have kept my Father's commandments and abide in his love. These things I have spoken to you, that my joy may be in you, and that your joy may be full" (John 15:10–11).
- *To experience God's favor.* "A good man obtains favor from the LORD, but a man of evil devices he condemns" (Prov. 12:2).
- *Our union with Christ.* "For if we have been united with him in a death like his, we shall certainly be united with him in a resurrection like his. We know that our old self was crucified with him in order that the body of sin might be brought to nothing, so that we would no longer be enslaved to sin" (Rom. 6:5–6).

As exhausting as this list might be, it could easily be doubled or tripled. God doesn't command obedience "just cuz." He gives us dozens of specific reasons to be holy. God can prescribe many different medicines for motivation. If you're struggling with pornography, he might call to mind your identity in Christ or admonish you that the sexually immoral will not inherit the kingdom of God. If you are fighting pride, God might assure you that he gives grace to the humble or remind you that you follow a crucified Messiah. He can highlight your adoption, justification, reconciliation, or union with Christ. God can stir you up to love and good deeds with warnings and promises, with love and fear, with positive or negative examples. He can remind you of who you are, or who you were, or who you are becoming. God can appeal to your good, the good of others, or his own glory. You could probably find a hundred biblical reasons to be holy. And the sooner we explore and apply those reasons, the more equipped we'll be to fight sin, the more eager to make every effort to be more like Christ, and the more ready to say with the apostle John, "his commandments are not burdensome" (1 John 5:3).

Chapter Five

THE PLEASURE OF GOD AND THE POSSIBILITY OF GODLINESS

One of my greatest joys in ministry is serving alongside my fellow elders. The leaders I get to work with at my church are wonderful examples of grace and godly maturity. Even when we have hard things on the agenda (which is often), I always look forward to our meetings. The work is good, the discussions are sharpening, the fellowship is sweet.

And usually there are cookies and donuts.

Because these men are godly, they are humble. This humility inevitably shows through when we talk about the scriptural qualifications for eldership in 1 Timothy 3 and Titus 1. The elders, and those training to be elders, often feel inadequate compared to the New Testament standards. The requirements seem like good goals, but in the end, lofty ideals that they won't ever reach.

When these objections come up, I try to tell the men that I agree with them sort of, but not really. It's appropriate for us to admit, "I'm not always gentle. I have been quarrelsome before. I'm not as hospitable as I'd like to be. My household doesn't always feel well managed." No one is perfect. So in that way none of us can live up to the Bible's depiction of holiness—not the elders, not the pastor, not John Stott or Billy Graham. But why do we think the qualifications for eldership entail absolute perfection? Surely

Paul gave these instructions because he thought some men would be recognized as meeting these requirements. He wasn't asking for sinless messiahs, but he expected that some men in the church would be examples of the qualities he outlined.

I imagine we all know people we think are "holy" even if we wouldn't dare give ourselves the label. In one sense, that's admirable humility. It's never a good sign when you meet someone eager to regale you with tales of his eminent holiness. But this kind of caution can easily lead us to the unbiblical conclusion that godliness is not actually possible, that we cannot keep the law in any respect. It's one thing to be humble about our piety. It's another to think piety is impossible. The truth is God's people *can* be righteous—not perfectly, but truly, and in a way that genuinely pleases God.

A GOSPEL-CENTERED PANCAKE

With all the best intentions, we tend to flatten the biblical view on holiness until we squeeze out the dynamic nature of life with God. In an effort to own up to our own abiding sinfulness and highlight the gospel of free grace, we remove any notion that we can obey God or that he can delight in our good works. So we end up believing something like this:

> I am a spiritual failure, but, praise God, Jesus came to save spiritual failures like me! I cannot obey God's commands for one nanosecond. I never truly love God with all my heart or my neighbor as myself. Even my righteous deeds are like filthy rags. If you could see my heart, you'd see that my sins are as bad as anyone else's or worse! I am a spiritual screw-up through and through, unfaithful to my faithful God. But the good news is, God has saved me because of Christ's death and resurrection. I am his adopted child, forgiven and clean. Nothing I ever do can make God love me any more—or any less—than he already loves me in Christ. Even though I con-

tinue to sin, I can never disappoint my heavenly Father, for he looks at me and sees the righteousness of his beloved Son. What unspeakable good news!

"So what's wrong with this?" you may ask incredulously. Well, as a general statement confessing sin and clinging to the righteousness of Christ, it is absolutely true and beautiful. If I heard a paragraph like this my first reaction would be to praise God for such a powerful reminder of gospel grace. But if someone asked me to probe deeper, I'd caution that this statement is not very careful. And where our theology is not careful, our Christian lives are often adversely affected. In this case, the theological confusion can short-circuit a passionate pursuit of personal holiness.

IMAGINE THE POSSIBILITIES

If we are to be passionate in our pursuit of personal holiness, the first thing we must establish is that holiness is possible. It sounds humble to say, "I cannot obey God for one nanosecond in my life," but it's not true. Acting like holiness is out of reach for the ordinary Christian doesn't do justice to the way the Bible speaks about people like Zechariah and Elizabeth, who "were both righteous before God, walking blamelessly in all the commandments and statutes of the Lord" (Luke 1:6). It doesn't take seriously the Lord's commendation of Job as "a blameless and upright man, who fears God and turns away from evil" (Job 1:8). And there's Paul, who frequently commends his churches and his ministry partners for their obedience and godly example. It sure seems like holiness is a possibility for God's people.

Likewise, Jesus teaches that the wise person hears his words and does them (Matt. 7:24). James says the same thing (James 2:22–25). There's no hint that doing God's word was only a hypothetical category. Quite the contrary, we are told to disciple the nations so that they might *obey* everything Jesus commanded (Matt. 28:19–20).

God expects the Christian to be marked by virtues like love, joy, and peace (Gal. 5:22–23) instead of being known for sexual immorality, idolatry, theft, and greed (1 Cor. 6:9–11). The Christian should no longer be trapped in habitual lawlessness (1 John 3:4). "By this it is evident who are the children of God, and who are the children of the devil: whoever does not practice righteousness is not of God, nor is the one who does not love his brother" (1 John 3:10). God expects us to be holy and gives us the grace to be holy. After all, he created us for good works (Eph. 2:10), and he works in us to will and to work for his good pleasure (Phil. 2:13). Christians *can* be rich in good works (1 Tim. 6:18; Acts 9:36). We *can* walk in a way worthy of our calling (Eph. 4:1). We *can* be trained to live in a way that is holy and acceptable to God (Rom. 12:1–2).

A PERFECT STORM

If the possibility of holiness is so plain in the Bible, why do we find it so hard to believe? Probably the biggest reason is because we equate obedience with perfection. If walking in a worthy manner means I never lose my temper, I never lust, I am never lazy, and I never do any good thing with mixed motives, well then of course holiness is impossible. Likewise, if God-pleasing holiness means I have to be filled to the brim with every virtue, without any room for improvement, I'm wasting my time even attempting to be holy. Expecting perfection from ourselves or others is not what holiness is about.

Does it ever feel like you don't have enough hours in the day to obey God? I feel that all the time. I don't mind the "do not" commands. They seem reasonable. I don't have to block off time in my day *not* to murder someone. But I get hung up on all that seems to be required of me to be a great dad, a super husband, a fabulous prayer warrior, a tremendous evangelist, and a devoted social activist. I always feel like I could pray more; I could evangelize more; I could share my resources more. But God doesn't expect us to be the best in everything in order to be free from paralyzing guilt. As we saw in chapter 2, it's our Christlike character that counts.

"Sounds great," you might say, "but have you seen my character? It's not without a few pimples." I know the feeling. I've never had a day where I felt kind enough, joyful enough, or loving enough. And if I ever have a day where I feel I've accomplished everything in the previous sentence, it's probably a pretty good sign that either I'm extremely far from holiness . . . or I'm in heaven.

But God does not expect our good works to be flawless in order for them to be good. If God only accepted perfect obedience from his children, the Bible would have nothing good to say about Job or David or Elizabeth or anyone else except for Jesus. I like what the Westminster Confession of Faith says about good works. On the one hand, sanctification will always be imperfect in this life. There will always be remnants of corruption in us. But by the power of the sanctifying Spirit of Christ, true believers will genuinely grow in grace. Our good works are accepted by God, not because they are "wholly unblameable and unreproveable in God's sight," but because God is pleased through Christ to accept our sincere obedience, although it contains many weaknesses and imperfections.[1] God not only works obedience in us by his grace, it's also by his grace that our imperfect

---

[1] The points in the last three sentences correspond to Westminster Confession 13.2, 13.3, and 16.6 respectively.

obedience is acceptable in his sight. And even the smallest act of obedience is an event worth celebrating. Perhaps we are slow to see any good in us because we don't understand how bad we were. Your tiny spiritual life may seem less negligible when you consider that it comes from a heart that used to be spiritually dead. That you and I have any law-abiding willing and doing is a miracle of God's grace.

FILTHY RAGS OR FULLY PLEASING?

Many Christians believe that all their righteous deeds are nothing but filthy rags. After all, that's what Isaiah 64:6 seems to say: even your best deeds are dirty and worthless. But I don't think this is what Isaiah means. The "righteous deeds" Isaiah has in mind are most likely the perfunctory rituals offered by Israel without sincere faith and without wholehearted obedience. In Isaiah 65:1–7 the Lord rejects Israel's sinful sacrifices. They are an insult to the Lord, smoke in his nostrils, just like the ritual "obedience" of Isaiah 58 that did not impress the Lord because his people were oppressing the poor. Their "righteous deeds" were "filthy rags" (64:6, KJV) because they weren't righteous at all. They looked good but were a sham, a literal smoke screen to cover up their unbelief and disobedience.

But we should not think that every kind of "righteous deed" is like a filthy rag before God. In fact the previous verse, Isaiah 64:5, says "you [God] meet him who joyfully *works righteousness*, those who remember you in your ways." It is not impossible for God's people to commit righteous acts that please God. John Piper explains:

> Sometimes people are careless and speak disparagingly of all human righteousness, as if there were no such thing that pleased God. They often cite Isaiah 64:6 which says our righteousness is

as filthy rags. It is true–gloriously true–that none of God's people, before or after the cross, would be accepted by an immaculately holy God if the perfect righteousness of Christ were not imputed to us (Romans 5:19; 1 Corinthians 1:30; 2 Corinthians 5:21). But that does not mean that God does not produce in those "justified" people (before and after the cross) an experiential righteousness that is not "filthy rags." In fact, he does; and this righteousness is precious to God and is required, not as the ground of our justification (which is the righteousness of Christ only), but as an evidence of our being truly justified children of God.[2]

It is a dangerous thing to ignore the Bible's assumption, and expectation, that righteousness is possible. Of course, our righteousness can never appease God's wrath. We need the imputed righteousness of Christ. More than that, we cannot produce any righteousness in our own strength. But as born-again believers, it is possible to please God by his grace. Those who bear fruit in every good work and increase in the knowledge of God are fully pleasing to God (Col. 1:10). Presenting your body as a living sacrifice pleases God (Rom. 12:1). Looking out for your weaker brother pleases God (14:18). Obeying your parents pleases God (Col. 3:20). Teaching the Word in truth pleases God (1 Thess. 2:4). Praying for the governing authorities pleases God (1 Tim. 2:1–3). Supporting your family members in need pleases God (5:4). Sharing with others pleases God (Heb. 13:16). Keeping his commandments pleases God (1 John 3:22). Basically, whenever you trust and obey, God is pleased.[3]

We can think it's a mark of spiritual sensitivity to consider everything we do as morally suspect. But this is not the way the Bible thinks about righteousness. More importantly, this kind of spiritual resignation does not tell the truth about God. A. W. Tozer is right:

> From a failure to properly understand God comes a world of unhappiness among good Christians even today. The Christian life is thought to be a glum, unrelieved cross-carrying under the eye of a stern Father who expects much and excuses nothing. He is austere, peevish, highly temperamental and extremely hard to please.[4]

But this is no way to view the God of the Bible. Our God is not a capricious slave driver. He is not hyper-sensitive and prone to fits of rage on account of slight offenses. He is slow to anger and abounding in steadfast love (Ex. 34:6). "He is not hard to please," Tozer reminds us, "though He may be hard to satisfy."[5]

Why do we imagine God to be so unmoved by our heart-felt attempts at obedience? He is, after all, our heavenly *Father*. What sort of father looks at his daughter's homemade birthday card and complains that the color scheme is all wrong? What kind of mother says to her son, after he gladly cleaned the garage but put the paint cans on the wrong shelf, "This is worthless in my sight"? What sort of parent rolls his eyes when his child falls off the bike on the first try? There is no righteousness that makes us right with God except for the righteousness of Christ. But for those who have been made right with God by grace alone through faith alone and therefore have been adopted into God's family, many of our righteous deeds are not only *not* filthy in God's eyes, they are exceedingly sweet, precious, and pleasing to him.

THE HAZARD OF MORAL EQUIVALENCE

There are two other confusions about sanctification we need to clear up in this chapter. The first is the mistaken notion that every

---

[4]A. W. Tozer, *The Best of A. W. Tozer, Volume 1* (Grand Rapids, MI: Baker, 1978), 121.
[5]Ibid.

sin is the same in God's eyes. This sentiment is popular with many Christians. For some it's a sign of genuine humility—"I deserve God's wrath too. So how can I judge your mistakes?" For others this is a way to dodge the hits that come when you dare to speak out against certain sins—"Yes, I do think homosexuality is wrong, but it's no worse than any other sin." And for still others, it's simply a soft form of relativism—"Those who live in glass houses shouldn't throw stones, you know."

Like many popular adages, this one about all sins being equal before God is not entirely wrong. Every sin is a breach of God's holy law. And whoever fails to keep the law in one point is guilty of breaking all of it (James 2:10). So any sin committed against an infinite God deserves punishment. We're all born sinners. We all sin. Every sin deserves death. That's why the truism is half-true.

But it's also a lot not true. As R. C. Sproul puts it, "The idea of gradation of sin is important for us to keep in mind so we understand the difference between *sin* and *gross sin*."[6] All our sins are offensive to God and require forgiveness. But over and over the Bible teaches that some sins are worse than others.

- God waited four hundred years before giving the Israelites the Promised Land because the iniquity of the Amorites was not yet complete (Gen. 15:16). They were sinners all along, but eventually their sins merited drastic punishment.
- The Mosaic legislation prescribes different penalties for different infractions and requires different sacrifices and payments to make restitution.
- Numbers 15 recognizes the difference between unintentional sins and those done "with a high hand" (Num. 15:29–30). Dropping a four-letter word when you hit your thumb with a hammer is

---

[6]Sproul, *Holiness of God*, 206 (emphasis his). See also the Westminster Larger Catechism, Q/A 150, which explains that, "All transgressions of the law of God are not equally heinous; but some sins in themselves, and by reason of several aggravations, are more heinous in the sight of God than others." The next question and answer details what those "aggravations" are.

not as bad as giving God the middle finger (though neither is recommended).

- Some sins in Israel's history were more notorious than others. Judging from the Lord's outrage, sacrificing your children to Molech was probably worse than losing your patience with them (Jer. 32:35).
- Jesus intimates that some people will be judged more severely on the day of judgment because they had more reason to believe (Matt. 10:15). We will all be judged according to the light we have.
- Though not saved by his good works, Cornelius was nevertheless "a devout man who feared God" (Acts 10:2). Even among non-Christians there is a difference between being a decent human being and being a dirty, rotten scoundrel.

Here's the problem: when every sin is seen as the same, we are less likely to fight any sins at all. Why should I stop sleeping with my girlfriend when there will still be lust in my heart? Why pursue holiness when even one sin in my life means I'm Osama bin Hitler in God's eyes? Again, it seems humble to act as if no sin is worse than another, but we lose the impetus for striving and the ability to hold each other accountable when we tumble down the slip-n-slide of moral equivalence. All of a sudden the elder who battles the temptation to take a second look at the racy section of the Lands' End catalog shouldn't dare exercise church discipline on the young man fornicating with reckless abandon. When we can no longer see the different gradations among sins and sinners and sinful nations, we have not succeeded in respecting our own badness; we've cheapened God's goodness. If our own legal system does not treat all infractions in the same way, surely God knows that some sins are more heinous than others. If we can spot the difference, we'll be especially eager to put to death those sins which are most offensive to God.

SONS, NOT ILLEGITIMATE CHILDREN

The second confusion that needs clearing up is whether or not forgiven, justified, reconciled, adopted, born-again believers can displease God. The logic seems sound: "I am clothed in Christ's righteousness. Nothing can separate me from the love of God. So no matter what I do, God sees me as his pure, spotless child." It's true that there is no condemnation for those who are in Christ Jesus (Rom. 8:1), but this does not mean God will condone all our thoughts and behaviors. Though in Christ he overlooks our sins in a judicial sense, he is not blind to them.[7]

Scripture is clear that God is displeased when his people sin. We can "grieve" the Holy Spirit of God (Eph. 4:30). Though God is always for us in Christ (Rom. 8:31–34), Christ can still have things against us (Rev. 2:4). The fact that God disciplines his children (Heb. 12:7) means he can sometimes be displeased with them. But there's a flip side too. The fact that God disciplines his children means he loves us enough to correct us. If God never took note of our sin, he would never discipline. And if he left us without discipline, we would be illegitimate children and not true sons (v. 8). Love does not equal unconditional affirmation. Love entails the relentless pursuit of what is for our good. And our good is always growth in godliness. "Those whom I love," Jesus said to the church at Laodicea, "I reprove and discipline, so be zealous and repent" (Rev. 3:19).

Maybe this theological distinction will help. Through faith we are joined to Christ and have union with him. That bond is unbreakable. Our union with Christ is an established fact, guaranteed for all

---

[7] See, for example, John Flavel's *A Blow at the Root of Antinomianism* (1691). Flavel lists ten errors made by the anti-law men of his day. They include: "That God sees no sin in believers, whatsoever sins they commit" (Error 5); "That God is not angry with the elect, nor doth he smite them for their sins" (Error 6); and "That believers need not fear either their own sins, or the sins of others" (Error 8). Found online at http://www.truecovenanter.com/gospel/flavel_blow_at_the_root.html (accessed July 11, 2011).

eternity by the indwelling of the Spirit. When we sin, our *union* with Christ is not in jeopardy. But our *communion* is. It is possible for believers to have more or less of God's favor. It is possible for us to have sweet fellowship with God, and it's possible to experience his frown—not a frown of judgment, but a "for-us" frown that should spur us on to love and good deeds (Heb. 10:24).[8] I love John Calvin's phrase that God, while not ceasing to love his children, can still be "wondrously angry" toward them. God will never hate us, but he will mercifully frighten us with his wrath so that we might "shake off our sluggishness."[9] God disciplines us for our good, so that we may share his holiness (12:10). As the Westminster Confession of Faith puts it, those fully and irrevocably justified "may by their sins come under God's fatherly displeasure and not have a sense of His presence with them until they humble themselves, confess their sins, ask for forgiveness, and renew their faith in repentance" (Westminster Confession 11.5).

One of the main motivations for obedience is the pleasure of God. If we, in a well-intentioned effort to celebrate the unimpeachable nature of our justification, make it sound as though God no longer concerns himself with our sins, we'll put a choke on our full-throttle drive to holiness. God is our heavenly Father. He has adopted us by his grace. He will always love his true children. But if we are his true children we will also love to please him. It will be our delight to delight in him and know that he is delighting in us.

FEELING CLEAN

Perhaps you started the chapter feeling encouraged that holiness is actually possible. It was a welcome relief to learn that many of our righteous deeds are not filthy at all. But now you're back in

---

[8]See Grudem, "Pleasing God," 283–292.
[9]*Institutes* 3.2.12.

Eeyore mode, worried that your whole justified life will be a disappointment to God (and that you'll never find your tail). I don't want to leave you feeling discouraged—convicted perhaps, but not despondent. Yes, we can grieve the Spirit (Eph. 4:30), but the normal state for the Christian should be one of blessing and enjoying God's favor (which, by the way, is not the same as health, wealth, and prosperity).

I quote from the Puritans a lot in this book because they are powerful examples of pursuing holiness. And yet, I have to admit that Puritanism at its worst could be overly introspective and unnecessarily punishing on the conscience. If you try hard enough you can find idols of the heart lurking behind every good deed. Some Christians are prone to go on lengthy idol hunts and can't feel good unless they feel bad about something. That's why I tell my congregation at times, "You don't have to feel conviction for every sermon. Some of you are actually obedient and faithful in this area." Not perfectly, of course, but truly and sincerely.

At the end of 2 Corinthians Paul challenges his readers to, "Examine yourselves, to see whether you are in the faith" (2 Cor. 13:5). Many of us take this as a stern warning to figure out if we are real believers. And no doubt some of us need the wake-up call. But look at what Paul says next in that verse: "Test yourselves," he says. "Or do you not realize this about yourselves, that Jesus Christ is in you?" See, the so-called super-apostles were beating up on Paul, telling the Corinthians he was a ministerial misfit (see 2 Cor. 11:1–15). In response, Paul tells the Corinthians to look at themselves. "Hey guys, I am your minister, right? And you're Christians, right? Examine yourselves. You'll see that you are in the faith and I've been faithful." Paul challenged the Corinthians to examine themselves *because he expected them to pass the test.*

Of all the crazy things Paul said, 1 Corinthians 4:4 may be the most jolting. Here's the apostle Paul—Mr. Wretched Man That I Am, Mr. There Is No One Good, No Not One—and he tells the Corinthians, "I am not aware of anything against myself." Seriously?! You can't think of anything, Paul? Not a single idol buried somewhere under ten layers of your subconscious? Now let's not miss the next line: "but I am not thereby acquitted. It is the Lord who judges me." So Paul isn't claiming to be okay just because he feels okay. But he is saying he has a clear conscience. He obeys God and sticks close to his Word. This doesn't mean he's perfect. No doubt, he's bringing his sins daily before the Lord to be cleansed from all unrighteousness (1 John 1:8–9; Matt. 6:12). But he's not walking around feeling like a spiritual loser. He's not burdened with constant low-level guilt because he's not doing enough or because he detected a modicum of pride over lunch.

What's the secret to such freedom? Paul is not summoning the power of positive thinking or feeling good because he's got some judgment-free God. No, the reason for Paul's confidence is directly related to his character. As a general rule, holiness is his lifestyle. And as a godly man, he's getting along well with God. I think this is what 1 Thessalonians 3:13 means when it says that God will "establish your hearts blameless in holiness before our God and Father, at the coming of our Lord Jesus with all his saints." Paul is not talking about positional holiness at this point, but about progressive holiness, which is why verse 12 speaks of the Lord making us "*increase* and abound in love for one another and for all." God's children will never be as pristinely and unfailingly holy as God, but we should be holy. Christians should display a consistent pattern of obedience, along with a quick habit of going to God for cleansing when they are disobedient. This is how we can be established "blameless in holiness" and have the same confidence Paul enjoyed in 1 Corinthians 4.

The Bible clearly teaches that holiness is possible. This is good news, not bad news. You have permission to see evidences of grace in your life. You are allowed (and expected) to be obedient. You will never be perfect in this life. You cannot do anything to earn God's love. But as a redeemed, regenerate child of God you don't have to be a spiritual failure. By the mercies of God you can "present your bodies as a living sacrifice, holy and acceptable to God, which is your spiritual worship" (Rom. 12:1).

Chapter Six

SPIRIT-POWERED, GOSPEL-DRIVEN, FAITH-FUELED EFFORT

There are few things in life as unenlightening as the postgame interview. Don't get me wrong, they aren't always bad. Some athletes and coaches can be quite insightful. I've seen real poise and humility in some of these interviews. But in general you don't expect to hear original insights surface thirty seconds after the game has ended. What you do expect is a lot of talk about how we never gave up, how we always believed in ourselves, how we gave it 110 percent, and how these kids deserve all the credit in the world (really? all of it? the whole world? no credit left for anyone else?). Part of the problem is that interviewers usually ask inane questions: "You caught the pass at midfield, slipped past the safety, and then sprinted to the pylon—take us through your thoughts." What thoughts do you expect the slot receiver to have at that point? Probably something like, "Run faster." It's not as if he's going to deconstruct Dostoevsky.

The pregame interviews aren't much better. There you'll hear a lot about playing within ourselves, winning the turnover battle, taking it one game at a time, and other revolutionary sports strategies. It's not that any of these remarks are wrong. At one point they may have communicated something meaningful. But over time, and with overuse, bromides like "keeping your head in the game" and "not forcing it" became so common and so generic that they didn't say much of anything at all. Has it been the aim of any team ever in the history of sports anywhere to keep their head in the clouds and take it three games at a time?

Unfortunately, Christians can speak in the same generalities. Again, it's not that we are saying false things (not usually). We just aren't digging deep enough to see what makes the true advice true. "Give it over to God" may be wise counsel, but what does that mean? How exactly do we give something over to him? Or someone else may tell you to "believe in the promises of God." Yes, that's true, but which promises? And how do those promises help me do the right thing right now?

It's possible to be completely biblical and still less than helpful—especially when it comes to pursuing holiness. Most Christians know that sanctification is about God working in us as we work out our salvation with fear and trembling (Phil. 2:12–13). Hopefully we would all agree with John Owen that trying to be holy "from a self-strength, carried on by ways of self-invention, unto the end of a self-righteousness, is the soul and substance of all false religion in the world."[1] It would be a big mistake to think justification is all about God and sanctification is all about us. We want to work and serve and speak, not in our own strength but in the strength that God supplies (1 Pet. 4:11).

And yet, it's not immediately obvious what all this practically means. How does God work in us as we work this out? How can we serve in God's strength and not our own? Or more to the point of this chapter, what does it mean that our effort toward holiness should be "Spirit-powered, gospel-driven, and faith-fueled?" It's one thing to suggest that holiness comes when we "let the Spirit

---

[1] John Owen, *The Mortification of Sin* (Fearn, Ross-shire, UK: Christian Focus, 1996), 23.

work in us" or by "letting the gospel grip our hearts" or by "fighting to believe the good news of God's grace" or by "running to Jesus"—but how does any of this actually work? How does God use the Spirit, the gospel, and faith to make the possibility of holiness a reality?

HOLINESS BY HOLY SPIRIT POWER

It makes sense that the *Holy* Spirit would have a big role in making us holy. According to 1 Peter 1:2, we are saved "according to the foreknowledge of God the Father, in the sanctification of the Spirit," that we might be obedient to Jesus Christ and sprinkled by his blood. Sanctification in this verse has two senses. The Spirit sets us apart *in Christ* so that we might be cleansed by his blood (definitive sanctification), and he works *in us* so that we can be obedient to Jesus Christ (progressive sanctification). Through the Spirit we are given a new position and infused with a new power. Or to put it in Pauline language, since we are no longer in the flesh but in the Spirit, by the same Spirit we ought to put to death the deeds of the flesh (Rom. 8:9–13).[2]

But this brings us back to the practical question: how *does* the Spirit work in us to make us holy? One of the ways is to strengthen us with power in our "inner being" (Eph. 3:16). The work of the Spirit is often connected with power (Acts 1:8; Rom. 15:19; 1 Cor. 2:4; 1 Thess. 1:5). This power can manifest itself in signs and wonders, in spiritual gifts to edify the body, and in the ability to bear spiritual fruit. The same Spirit who was present at creation and caused you to be born again is at work to empower your inner person (that is, your will or heart) so that you might

---

[2] See Kevin DeYoung, *The Holy Spirit*, The Gospel Coalition Booklets, ed. D. A. Carson and Timothy Keller (Wheaton, IL: Crossway, 2010), 18–19. This section on the Spirit repeats some of the same points and a few of the same sentences in this earlier work.

resist sins you couldn't resist before and do the good things which would otherwise be impossible. Defeatist Christians who do not fight against sins because they figure they were "born this way" or "will never change" or "don't have enough faith" are not being humble. They dishonor the Holy Spirit who strengthens us with supernatural power.

But that's not all the Spirit does to sanctify us. The Spirit is power, but he is also a light. He shines into the dark places of our hearts and convicts us of sin (John 16:7–11). He is a lamp to illumine God's Word, teaching what is true and showing it to be precious (1 Cor. 2:6–16). And the Spirit throws a spotlight on Christ so that we can see his glory and be changed (John 16:14). That's why 2 Corinthians 3:18 says, "And we all, with unveiled face, beholding the glory of the Lord, are being transformed into the same image from one degree of glory to another. For this comes from the Lord who is the Spirit." Just as Moses had his face transformed when he saw the Lord's glory on Mount Sinai (Ex. 34:29; cf. 2 Cor. 3:7), so will we be transformed when, by the Spirit, we behold God's glory in the face of Christ.

To summarize, then, the Spirit is a light to us in three ways. (1) He exposes sin so that we can recognize it and turn away. (2) He illumines the Word so that we can understand its meaning and grasp its implications. (3) He takes the veil away so that we can see the glory of Christ and become what we behold. Or to put it another way, the Spirit sanctifies by revealing sin, revealing truth, and revealing glory. When we close our eyes to this light, the Bible calls it resisting the Spirit (Acts 7:51), or quenching (1 Thess. 5:19) or grieving the Spirit (Eph. 4:30). There may be slight nuances among the three terms, but they all speak of situations where we do not accept the Spirit's sanctifying work in our lives. If we give in to sin or give up on righteousness, the fault is not with the Spirit's power but with our preference for the darkness of evil rather than the Spirit's light (John 3:19–20).

GOOD DEEDS BASED ON GOOD NEWS

It seems almost every Christian I talk with these days insists that personal holiness will flow from a true grasp of the gospel. That's right, in so far as it goes. It just doesn't go far enough. We need to be more specific. How exactly do good deeds spring up from good news?

Let me suggest a couple of ways.

First, the gospel encourages godliness out of a sense of gratitude. This is the thought behind Romans 12:1–2. In view of God's mercies on display in Romans 1–11 (e.g., justification, adoption, predestination, atonement, reconciliation, preservation, glorification), our grateful response should be obedience to the imperatives in chapters 12–16. As John Stott remarks, "It is not by accident that in Greek one and the same noun (*charis*) does duty for both 'grace' and 'gratitude.'"[3]

Of course, we must be careful not to think of gratitude as some kind of debtor's ethic, as if God showed us mercy and now expects us to make up for it with a lifetime of quid pro quo obedience. We cannot repay God for anything (Rom. 11:35). But if we understand all that God has done for us in Christ, we will be happy and eager to please him. I get a lot of things wrong as a husband, but I've managed to get my wife some pretty good gifts. They usually involve some combination of time away from the kids and flying her mom out to save our sanity. When my wife receives a thoughtful gift like this (as opposed to, say, a gym membership), I'm usually sitting pretty for the rest of the day. That's not why

---

[3]John Stott, *Romans: God's Good News for the World* (Downer's Grove, IL: InterVarsity Press, 1994), 321.

I give the gift (really, Honey, it's not!), but a season (or more) of joyful gratitude is my kind wife's natural response. And besides, when we are grateful, we're not only eager to please God, we're less likely to get bogged down in ungodliness. The humility and happiness that come with thankfulness tend to crowd out what is coarse, ugly, or mean (Eph. 5:4).[4]

Second, the gospel aids our pursuit of holiness by telling us the truth about who we are.[5] Certain sins become more difficult when we understand our new position in Christ. If we are heirs to the whole world, why should we envy? If we are God's treasured possession, why be jealous? If God is our Father, why be afraid? If we are dead to sin, why live in it? If we've been raised with Christ, why continue in our old sinful ways? If we are seated in the heavenly places, why act like the devil of hell? If we are loved with an everlasting love, why are we trying to prove our worth to the world? If Christ is all in all, why am I so preoccupied with myself?

This last paragraph is what Martyn Lloyd-Jones called talking to yourself instead of listening to yourself.[6] It's easy to become convinced that we can never change or that God is ready to kick us to the curb after we've screwed up in the same way for the millionth time. But don't listen to yourself; preach to yourself. Go back to the gospel. Remember that there is therefore now no condemnation for those who are in Christ Jesus (Rom. 8:1). Remember that the Spirit of him who raised Jesus from the dead dwells in you (v. 11). Remember that you are a child of God, and if a child then an heir (vv. 16–17). Remember that nothing can separate us from

---

[4]John Piper, *Future Grace* (Sisters, OR: Multnomah, 1995), 48. It should be noted that in general Piper is cautious about gratitude-based obedience because he fears it slides into a debtor's ethic.
[5]I'll say much more about this in chapter 8.
[6]See, for example, Martyn Lloyd-Jones *Spiritual Depression: Its Causes and Cures* (Grand Rapids, MI: Eerdmans, 1965), 20.

the love of God that is in Christ Jesus our Lord (vv. 38–39). God gives more grace (James 4:6). Draw near to him, recognize who you are in him, and keep on working to cleanse your hands and purify your hearts (v. 8).

STANDING ON THE PROMISES

Faith is central to Christianity. We get that. Justification comes by faith apart from works of the law (Rom. 3:28). But what role is there for faith after we are saved? Is the hard struggle to grow in holiness removed from the exercise of faith?

May it never be!

By faith we are justified. And by faith we make every effort to be sanctified. Faith is operative in both—in justification to receive and rest, and in sanctification to will and to work.

In a way, we've already talked about faith—trusting in the gospel and believing what the Bible says about our position in Christ. But in the pursuit of holiness we need to look at more than the past acts of redemption. We have to look forward and trust in "future grace."[7]

Justification is not the only remedy for sin. Understanding what God has done for us will not smash every idol. There are longings in our souls that will be satisfied only by the promise of future blessing. How else can we make sense of the *hope* of glory? God is constantly making promises in the Bible, and these promises are meant to fuel the engine of obedience.

Let me show you what I mean by briefly looking at one familiar section of Scripture—the Sermon on the Mount. These three chapters (Matthew 5–7) are filled with commands. They are also

---

[7]If you want the better, longer version of what I'm trying saying in a few paragraphs, read John Piper's book *Future Grace*. See also the smaller version *Battling Unbelief: Defeating Sin with Superior Pleasure* (Colorado Springs: Multnomah, 2007).

filled with promises—some of them promises of judgment, many of them promises of future grace. Start with the Beatitudes. They all promise blessing of one kind or another. The meek shall inherit the earth (Matt. 5:5). The persecuted will have the kingdom of heaven (v. 10). The reviled will receive a great reward (v. 12). In my experience, Matthew 5:8—"Blessed are the pure in heart, for they shall see God"—has been the most helpful verse in the Bible in battling the temptation to lust. The key is that Jesus fights pleasure with pleasure. Sexual impurity can be pleasing (in the moment), but Jesus promises a greater blessing for the pure of heart: they will see God. Years ago, there was a house in our neighborhood I often went past on my way to work. I don't know who lived there and never met anyone from the house. But frequently in the summer a young lady in an immodest bathing suit would wash the car in the driveway. Matthew 5:8 was the sword I used to slay my temptation to turn my head and take a look. I thought to myself, "I want to see God. I want to know God. I don't want to feel distant from him the rest of the day. I know fellowship with God is better than a three-second glance." I was pursuing holiness by faith in the promises of God.

And the promises continue throughout the world's most famous sermon. Many are warnings. If you murder, you'll be liable to judgment (Matt. 5:21), and whoever says, "you fool" will be liable to hell (v. 22). If you don't curb your lust, you can end up there too (vv. 29–30). Don't forgive, and you won't be forgiven (6:15). Walk down the easy path, and you'll face destruction (7:13). Build your house on the sand by ignoring Jesus' words, and your house will fall (7:26–27). These are all promises—albeit negative promises—meant to empower our obedience.

Jesus promises blessings too. If you uphold the commandments, you'll be great in the kingdom of heaven (Matt. 5:19). If you enter the narrow gate and walk down the hard path you'll find life (7:14). If you hear the words of Jesus and do them, you'll have true security (7:24–25). Jesus wants to motivate us by the thought of reward—real, eternal, lasting reward (6:1, 2, 4, 5, 6, 16, 18, 19–20). He understands that the fight against sin is a fight to trust in our heavenly Father. That's why worry is not just a personality quirk, but a sign of unbelief (v. 30). If we have faith in God's future grace, we will seek first the kingdom of God and trust that God will give us what we need (v. 33). Our Father promises to give good things to those who ask him (7:11).

As our covenant God, he guarantees blessing when we obey and threatens curses for disobedience. The blessings may not be what we expect and they may not come until the next life (Heb. 11:39–40), but they are always good and always for the ultimate end that we may become more like Christ (Rom. 8:28–29). The holy life is always a life of faith, believing with all our hearts that God will do what he has promised.

One last thing: I've been talking about faith in the gospel or faith in the promises of God, especially the promises of future grace. But we could also talk more broadly about faith in the Word of God. That's essentially what spiritual warfare is: believing the truth from God instead of the lies from the devil. Satan is the father of lies, and his basic weapon is deception. He lies about God. He lies about your sin. He lies about your forgiveness. He lies about the Bible. Resisting the devil has nothing to do with haunted houses or spinning heads. It has to do with faith, trusting in truth instead of lies. That's what Ephesians 6 is all about. Put on the belt of truth. Take up the shield of faith. Wield the sword of the Spirit. In spiritual warfare you stand fast against the schemes of the devil by standing fast on the Word of God.[8]

EFFORT IS NOT A FOUR-LETTER WORD

I would be remiss if I didn't finish this chapter by saying something about the last word in the chapter title. Yes, the Spirit empowers our pursuit of holiness. Yes, the gospel drives us toward Christlikeness. Yes, faith fuels our obedience. But we still put forth effort. God's mercy does not automatically produce obedience. We must be told to obey and then go do it.[9] God is the agent in our sanctification (1 Thess. 5:23). He is the one making us holy. But we must pursue what is God's gift to us. Or as John Piper puts it, "When it comes to killing my sin, I don't wait passively for the miracle of sin-killing to be worked on me, I act the miracle."[10]

It is the consistent witness of the New Testament that growth in godliness requires exertion on the part of the Christian. Romans 8:13 says that by the Spirit we must put to death the deeds of the flesh. Ephesians 4:22–24 instructs us to put off the old self and put on the new. Colossians 3:5 commands us to put to death what is earthly in us. First Timothy 6:12 urges us to fight the good fight. Luke 13:24 exhorts us to strive to enter the narrow gate. First Corinthians 9:24–27 speaks of running a race and disciplining the body. Philippians 3:12–14 talks of pressing on and straining forward. Second Peter 1:5 flat out commands us to "make every effort." Your part as a born-again believer is to "toil, struggling with all his energy" as Christ powerfully works within us (Col. 1:29). We must never forget that accord-

---

[8]The best book I know of on spiritual warfare—as the Bible understands it—is the old Puritan classic by Thomas Brooks, *Precious Remedies against Satan's Devices* (Edinburgh: Banner of Truth, 1997 [1652]).

[9]See Douglas J. Moo, *The Epistle to the Romans* (Grand Rapids, MI: Eerdmans, 1996), 749–750.

[10]http://www.desiringgod.org/blog/posts/i-act-the-miracle. Accessed July 15, 2011.

ing to Jesus the reward of eternal life goes to those who conquer and overcome (Revelation 2–3).

Christians work—they work to kill sin and they work to live in the Spirit. They have rest in the gospel, but never rest in their battle against the flesh and the devil. The child of God has two great marks about him: he is known for his inner warfare and his inner peace.[11] As gospel Christians, we should not be afraid of striving, fighting, and working. These are good Bible words. "No one can attain any degree of holiness without God working in his life," Jerry Bridges writes, "but just as surely no one will attain it without effort on his own part. God has made it possible for us to walk in holiness. But He has given us the responsibility of doing the walking."[12] Putting off the corruption of the flesh is, as Calvin put it, "a work arduous and of immense labor." Therefore, God "bids us to strive and make every effort for this purpose. He intimates that no place is to be given in this case to sloth."[13] When it comes to sanctification, we don't just look to the Lord. We don't just get gripped by the gospel. We also work hard to be holy.

Let's not make the mistake of the old Keswick theology with its "let go and let God" view of sanctification.[14] In *The Christian's Secret of a Happy Life* (an unfortunate classic from the Higher Life movement), Hannah Whitall Smith argues, "All that we claim then in this life of sanctification is that by a step of faith we put ourselves into the hands of the Lord, for Him to work in us all the good pleasure of His will; and that by a continuous exercise

---

[11]This is a paraphrase of a line from J. C. Ryle, *Holiness: Its Nature, Hindrances, Difficulties, and Roots* (Moscow, ID: Charles Nolan, 2011), 69.

[12]Jerry Bridges, *The Pursuit of Holiness* (Colorado Springs: NavPress, 2006), 10–11.

[13]Calvin's commentary on 2 Peter 1:5. See *Calvin's Commentaries Volume XXII*, ed. John Owen (Grand Rapids, MI: Baker, 1993), 372.

[14]The theology is so named because it was first promoted at conferences held in Keswick, England in the late nineteenth century. The conferences continue to this day, but one should not assume the theology is the same. At present, the conferences are on solid footing. For an excellent examination of the old Keswick movement and its theological problems see Andrew David Naselli, *Let Go and Let God? A Survey and Analysis of Keswick Theology* (Bellingham, WA: Logos Bible Software, 2010).

of faith we keep ourselves there. . . . Our part is trusting, it is His to accomplish the results."[15] This may sound super-spiritual, but it's not biblical. Sanctification is not by surrender, but by divinely enabled toil and effort.

Listen to Martyn Lloyd-Jones:

> The New Testament calls upon us to take action; it does not tell us that the work of sanctification is going to be done for us. . . . We are in the 'good fight of faith', and we have to do the fighting. But, thank God, we are enabled to do it; for the moment we believe, and are justified by faith, and are born again of the Spirit of God, we have the ability. So the New Testament method of sanctification is to remind us of that; *and having reminded us of it, it says, 'Now then, go and do it'.*[16]

This is why when one old Dutch theologian listed his "Reasons Why Believers Do Not Grow as Much as They Ought," he mentioned not only "gospel" reasons like doubting their conversion or presuming upon grace, he also included plain old laziness: "We indeed desire to be in an elevated spiritual frame and to grow as a palm tree, but we are not willing to exert any effort—and thus we also do not receive it."[17] Which is another way of saying there's no place for quietism in the quest for Christlikeness.

These issues matter because some Christians are stalled out in their sanctification for simple lack of effort. They need to know about the Spirit's power. They need to be rooted in gospel grace. They need to believe in the promises of God. And they need to fight, strive, and make every effort to work out all that God is working in them. Let us say with Paul, "I worked harder than any

[15]Hannah W. Smith, *The Christian's Secret of a Happy Life* (Gloucestershire, UK: Dodo Press, 2008 [1875]), 7.
[16]D. Martyn Lloyd-Jones, *Romans: Exposition of Chapter 6: The New Man* (Edinburgh: Banner of Truth, 1972), 178 (emphasis mine).
[17]Wilhelmus A Brakel, *The Christian's Reasonable Service*, trans. Bartel Elshout, ed. Joel R. Beeke, 4 vols. (Grand Rapids, MI: Reformation Heritage Books, 1994), 4:154.

of them, though it was not I, but the grace of God that is with me" (1 Cor. 15:10). Without this biblical emphasis, we'll be confused, wondering why sanctification isn't automatically flowing from a heartfelt commitment to gospel-drenched justification. We'll be waiting around for enough faith to really "get the gospel" when God wants us to get up and get to work (Phil. 2:12–13). Because when it comes to growth in godliness, trusting does not put an end to trying.

Chapter Seven

BE WHO YOU ARE

It was one of those fall days in Michigan perfect for playing in the backyard. A little cold, but just cold enough that it felt good to run around. I was playing soccer with my two oldest sons. Jacob, the younger of the two, was on my team against Ian, his older brother. After stopping Ian's shot on goal I motioned for Jacob to run to the other end of the yard for a long pass. As he started running, I kicked the ball with the inside of my right foot. The ball sailed past both sons and kept rolling . . . rolling . . . rolling, until it finally found its way into the goal at the other end of the yard. Ian was a bit deflated. Jacob, five years old at the time, was amazed. With a look of wonder on his face he turned to me and said in all seriousness, "Wow, Dad, only you and Jesus can do that."

I can't really speak to Jesus' abilities at soccer. I checked Wikipedia and didn't get many details. But I can say that my son's pronouncement would have been theological dynamite if he had only changed one word. See, most of us know we are supposed to be like Jesus. On our better days we even want to be like Jesus. We'd love for someone to look at our lives, see our godliness, and say, "Wow, only you and Jesus can do that."

This is not a bad sentiment. But the problem is with the word "and." That conjunction ought to be a preposition. "Only you *in* Jesus can do that." Christlikeness is possible, but not by merely working with Jesus or simply imitating his example.

Only by knowing our position *in* Jesus can we begin to live *like* Jesus.

JESUS CHRIST AND UNION STATION

The theological term for being in Jesus is "union with Christ." How this connects with holiness will become apparent soon enough, but first we need to put some theological meat on these bones, because most of us are mighty thin on this point of theology. Union with Christ may be the most important doctrine you've never heard of. As Christians, we know we've been saved by Christ, we should look like Christ, and we can have a relationship with Christ. But we almost never consider how all this depends on our union with Christ.

The whole of our salvation can be summed up with reference to this reality. Union with Christ is not a single specific blessing we receive in our salvation. Rather it is the best phrase to describe *all* the blessings of salvation, whether in eternity past (election), in history (redemption), in the present (effectual calling, justification, and sanctification), or in the future (glorification).[1]

Every blessing is received in Christ (Eph. 1:3). No aspect of our salvation can be excluded from our union with him. This is the foundation and basis for all his gifts. So while it's appropriate for theologians to talk about an "order of salvation" (*ordo salutis*), whereby we are called by the Spirit, born again, moved to faith and repentance, justified, adopted, sanctified, preserved, and glorified, we must never separate these benefits from the Benefactor. Every blessing in the order of salvation flows from our union with Christ. As John Murray said, "It is not simply a step in the application of redemption; when viewed, according to the teaching of Scripture,

---

[1] Michael Horton, *The Christian Faith: A Systematic Theology for Pilgrims On the Way* (Grand Rapids, MI: Zondervan, 2011), 587.

in its broader aspects it underlies every step of the application of redemption. Union with Christ is really *the central truth of the whole doctrine of salvation* not only in its application but also in its once-for-all accomplishment in the finished work of Christ."[2]

The doctrine of union with Christ is so common in the New Testament that you may have missed it. Over two hundred times in Paul's letters and more than two dozen times in the writings of John we see expressions like "in Christ," "in the Lord," or "in him."[3] We are found in Christ (Phil. 3:9), preserved in Christ (Rom. 8:39), saved and sanctified in Christ (2 Tim. 1:9; 1 Cor. 1:30). We walk in Christ (Col. 2:6), labor in Christ (1 Cor. 15:58), and obey in Christ (Eph. 6:1). We die in Christ (Rev. 14:13), live in Christ (Gal. 2:20), and conquer in Christ (Rom. 8:37)—just to name a few examples. Another thirty-two times Paul speaks of believers participating together with Christ in some aspect of redemption, whether it's being crucified with Christ, being buried with Christ, being raised with Christ, or being seated with Christ.[4] Apart from this kind of union, all the blessings of Christ would be outside us. It's only when the Spirit joins us to Christ and we are engrafted into his body that we can participate, not only in Christ's benefits, but in Christ himself.[5] The whole of the Christian life, from election to justification to sanctification to final glorification, is made

---

[2]John Murray, *Redemption—Accomplished and Applied* (Grand Rapids, MI: Eerdmans, 1955), 161 (emphasis mine). See also Robert Letham, *The Work of Christ* (Downers Grove, IL: InterVarsity Press, 1993), 80, 81; Sinclair Ferguson, *The Holy Spirit* (Downers Grove, IL: InterVarsity Press, 1997), 100, 106. Likewise, the Westminster Larger Catechism understands the "order of salvation" (*ordo salutis*) to be the outworking of our union with Christ (66, 69).

[3]Bruce Demarest, *The Cross and Salvation: The Doctrine of Salvation* (Wheaton, IL: Crossway, 2006), 313. According to Demarest, there are 216 occurrences of "in Christ" (and similar constructions) in Paul and twenty-six in John. Sinclair Ferguson puts the first number around 160 (*Holy Spirit*, 100).

[4]See Douglas J. Moo, *The Epistle to the Romans* (Grand Rapids, MI: Eerdmans, 1996), 392. See also Lane Tipton, "Union with Christ and Justification," in *Justified in Christ: God's Plan for Us in Justification*, ed. K. Scott Oliphint (Fearn, Ross-shire, UK: Mentor, 2007), 25. Both Moo and Tipton include numerous biblical references for "in Christ" and "with Christ" language.

[5]Theologians often speak of an "alien righteousness" in our justification. The idea is that we are saved by a righteousness not our own. While this is certainly true, the word "alien" can be misleading. For Christ is not alien to us but dwells within us.

possible by and is an expression of our union with Christ. That's why Jesus' final request in the High Priestly Prayer is that "I [may be] in them" (John 17:26) and why Paul says "Christ in you" is the hope of glory (Col. 1:27).

UNION CONFUSION

The doctrine of union with Christ has not played a prominent role in popular Christian thinking in recent years. The neglect is probably owing to a couple of factors. First, it can be hard to wrap your mind around this doctrine. After all, what exactly does it mean that we are joined to Christ or that he is in us and we are in him? Thinking spatially does not work. Christ isn't stapled to our side. He doesn't shrink-ray himself so that he can live like a microscopic organism in our left ventricle. The union isn't physical, but theological. Union with Christ implies three things: *solidarity* (Christ as the second Adam is our representative), *transformation* (Christ by the Holy Spirit changes us from the inside out), and *communion* (Christ abides with us as our God).[6] Union with Christ is like wedlock, where we are joined to Christ in a covenant of love. It is like a body where we as members are joined to our living Head. Or you might say union with Christ is like a building, where we are the house and Christ dwells within us. These biblical analogies are earthly ways of describing the heavenly reality of our union with Christ.

The other reason most Christians stay away from this doctrine is because it is easily misunderstood. Most basically, we must not equate union with fusion. The biblical teaching is that our person is joined to the person of Christ so that God is our God and we are his people. But this covenantal relationship is not the same as

---

[6]See Letham, *Work of Christ*, 82–83.

a fusion of natures. Our person does not dissolve into the person of Christ in an ontological union whereby the distinction between God and his people is eliminated.

Ontology is the fancy word for "being." So an ontological union would mean we actually share in the essence of God himself. For example, the medieval mystic Meister Eckhart said, "He who is one with God, is 'one spirit' with God, *the same existence*."[7] Surely this is not the right language. In certain strands of mysticism, not to mention Eastern religions, union with God is an Absolute Unity where two distinct beings are no longer distinct. But this is not what the Bible teaches about union with Christ. Just as the three persons of the Trinity share a union but are three distinct persons, and the two natures of Christ are united but remain distinct natures, so Christ has union with us without obliterating our own unique personhood. We do not become gods.

We can, however—in a certain sense—be deified. Second Peter 1:4 speaks of believers becoming "partakers of the divine nature." This language is strange to Western ears. And yet, deification (also called *theosis*) has always been central to an Eastern Orthodox understanding of salvation.[8] But Orthodox theology has been careful to distinguish between God's "essence" and his "energies."[9] We participate in the active life of God, not in the ineffable nature of God. Even Calvin said the purpose of the gospel is "to make us sooner or later like God; indeed it is, so to speak,

---

[7]Meister Eckhardt, *The Essential Sermons, Commentaries, Treatises, and Defence*, trans. and ed. Edmund Colledge and Bernard McGinn (Mahwah, NJ: Paulist Press, 1981), 56.

[8]Orthodoxy as a branch of Christianity is not to be confused with the term "orthodox," which refers to historic, biblical theology. The *ESV Study Bible* provides a good definition of Orthodoxy: "Orthodoxy comprises a range of autocephalous and autonomous churches, the Russian and Greek being the most prominent. During the first millennium A.D. the Latin West and the predominantly Greek-speaking East drifted apart linguistically, culturally, and theologically. Rome's claims to universal jurisdiction and its acceptance of the *filioque* clause in the Niceno-Constantinopolitan creed led to severed relations."

[9]See, for example, Kallistos Ware, *The Orthodox Way* (Crestwood, NY: St. Vladimir's Seminary Press, 1979), 21–23.

a kind of deification."[10] But he makes it clear that "deification" does not mean losing ourselves in God. Becoming like God means growing in the qualities and virtues of God. There is no mixture of human and divine. Our humanity is fully retained, but it is also set on a process of being fully restored. We cannot become God; but we can become like him.

The important point is that we do not think of spirituality as fundamentally an exercise in detachment from our soul so that we can fly to the sky and be absorbed into some Divine Absolute. We must always remember that union with Christ is possible because of the Son's descent to earth, not because of our ascent into heaven. The basis of our union with Christ is Christ's union with us in the incarnation. He became one with us so that we might become one with him. Christian spirituality does not rest on mysticism; it rests in a Mediator.

FROM BEING WITH CHRIST TO BEING LIKE CHRIST

I know this chapter has been more technical than the others, but the theological exploration is for good reason. Union with Christ is more than a fascinating doctrinal concept for bookworms and vocabulary junkies. It really matters for the way you live your life. It matters for your spiritual health. And it matters for your holiness.

There are several ways in which union with Christ guides our growth in godliness. For starters, it reminds us that the pursuit of holiness is also the pursuit of Christ. We aren't interested in being virtuous just to be good people. Our first love is Jesus. Holiness is not ultimately about living up to a moral standard. It's about living in Christ and living out of our real, vital union with him.

---

[10]*Calvin's Commentary*, 2 Peter 1:4. See *Calvin's Commentaries Volume XXII*, ed. John Owen (Grand Rapids, MI: Baker, 1993), 371.

Similarly, union with Christ helps put justification and sanctification in their proper relationship. There has been a tendency in theology and in the Christian life to view justification and sanctification in isolation. This leads some Christians to emphasize faith at the expense of works, or conversely, for other Christians to focus on our pursuit of righteousness apart from the imputed righteousness of Christ. But justification and sanctification are both "in Christ" gifts (1 Cor. 1:30; 6:11).

Theologians sometimes call this the double grace (*duplex gratia*) of union with Christ. They are two sides of the same coin, distinct yet joined. Calvin is right when he says about justification and sanctification, "those gifts of grace go together as if tied by an inseparable bond, so that if anyone tries to separate them, he is, in a sense, tearing Christ to pieces."[11] Sanctification doesn't just flow from justification, so that one produces the other. Both come from the same Source. Christ justifies no one whom he does not also sanctify. By virtue of our union with Christ, he bestows both gifts, the one never without the other. "Thus it is clear how true it is that we are justified *not without works* yet *not through works*, since in our sharing in Christ, which justifies us, [progressive] sanctification is just as much included as [imputed] righteousness."[12]

MAKING THE REALITY REAL

As important as these points are in connecting union with Christ and personal holiness, there is another connection much more

---

[11]*Calvin's* commentary on 1 Corinthians 1:30. See *Calvin's Commentaries Volume XX*, ed. John Pringle (Grand Rapids, MI: Baker, 1993), 93.

[12]*Institutes* 3.16.1 (emphasis mine). For more on Calvin's doctrine of union with Christ see William B. Evans, *Imputation and Impartation: Union with Christ in American Reformed Theology* (Eugene, OR: Wipf & Stock, 2008); Mark A. Garcia, *Life in Christ: Union with Christ and Twofold Grace in Calvin's Theology* (Eugene, OR: Wipf & Stock, 2008); J. Todd Billings, *Calvin, Participation, and the Gift: The Activity of Believers in Union with Christ* (Oxford: Oxford University Press, 2007); Richard B. Gaffin Jr., "Union with Christ: Some Biblical and Theological Reflections," in *Always Reforming: Explorations in Systematic Theology*, ed. A. T. B. McGowan (Downers Grove, IL: IVP Academic, 2007), 271–288.

prominent in the Bible. Our progress in the pursuit of holiness comes largely from understanding and appropriating our union with Christ. As John Murray states, "Nothing is more relevant to progressive sanctification than the reckoning of ourselves to be dead to sin and alive to God through Jesus Christ (cf. Rom. 6:11)."[13] Apart from our union with Christ every effort to imitate Christ, no matter how noble and inspired at the outset, inevitably leads to legalism and spiritual defeat. But once you understand the doctrine of union with Christ, you see that God doesn't ask us to attain to what we're not. He only calls us to accomplish what already is. The pursuit of holiness is not a quixotic effort to do just what Jesus did. It's the fight to live out the life that has already been made alive in Christ.

If I had to summarize New Testament ethics in one sentence, here's how I would put it: *be who you are*. That may sound strange, almost heretical, given our culture's emphasis on being true to yourself. But like so many of the worst errors in the world, this one represents a truth powerfully perverted. When people say, "Relax, you were born that way," or "Quit trying to be something you're not and just be the real you," they are stumbling upon something very biblical. God *does* want you to be the real you. He *does* want you to be true to yourself. But the "you" he's talking about is the "you" that you are by grace, not by nature. You may want to read through that last sentence again because the difference between living in sin and living in righteousness depends on getting that sentence right. God doesn't say, "Relax, you were born this way." But he does say, "Good news, you were reborn another way."

As a believer, you belong to Christ. More than that, you are

[13]John Murray, "The Pattern of Sanctification," in *Collected Writings of John Murray*, 4 vols. (Edinburgh: Banner of Truth, 1977), 2:311. See also Walter Marshall, *The Gospel Mystery of Sanctification: Growing in Holiness by Living in Union with Christ* (Eugene, OR: Wipf & Stock, 2005).

joined to Christ. By faith, through the Holy Spirit, we have union with him. Christ lives in you and you in him. You are one with Christ, so live like Christ. Be who you are. That's the consistent message of the New Testament:

- *In Christ, we are dead to sin and alive to righteousness.* "We were buried therefore with him by baptism into death, in order that, just as Christ was raised from dead by the glory of the Father, we too might walk in newness of life" (Rom. 6:4; cf. Col. 3:1–3).
- *In Christ, we are new creations so that we might live for him and not for ourselves.* "And he died for all, that those who live might no longer live for themselves but for him who for their sake died and was raised. . . . Therefore, if anyone is in Christ, he is a new creation. The old has passed away; behold, the new has come" (2 Cor. 5:15, 17).
- *In Christ, our sinful flesh is put to death and a new kind of life (a new Person, actually) is at work in us.* "I have been crucified with Christ. It is no longer I who live, but Christ who lives in me. And the life I now live in the flesh I live by faith in the Son of God, who loved me and gave himself for me" (Gal. 2:20).
- *In Christ, we are no longer sons of disobedience and children of wrath but are alive with Christ and able to do the good works prepared for us.* "But God, being rich in mercy, because of the great love with which he loved us, even when we were dead in our trespasses, made us alive together with Christ—by grace you have been saved—and raised us up with him and seated us with him in the heavenly places in Christ Jesus. . . . For we are his workmanship, created in Christ Jesus for good works, which God prepared beforehand, that we should walk in them" (Eph. 2:4–6, 10).
- *In Christ, we can walk as he did.* "Therefore, as you received Christ Jesus the Lord, so walk in him" (Col. 2:6).
- *In Christ, we are holy and precious and called to live like it.* "Put on then, as God's chosen ones, holy and beloved, compassionate hearts, kindness, humility, meekness, and patience, bearing with one another and, if one has a complaint against another, forgiving each other; as the Lord has forgiven you, so you also must forgive. And above all these put on love, which binds everything together in perfect harmony" (Col. 3:12–14).

Time after time, the Bible reminds us of our identity in Christ in order to call us to obedience to Christ. Do not strive after holiness because you cower in dread of God. Strive after holiness because you are confident you already belong to God.

THE OTHER ROMANS ROAD

Nowhere is the connection between union with Christ and sanctification clearer than in Romans 6. In this passage Paul is trying to answer the question "Are we to continue in sin that grace may abound?" He's just finished extolling justification by faith alone through grace alone in Christ alone. Now he anticipates an objection: if grace is so great, then we can all keep sinning (Rom. 6:1). "Hey, we can have the best of both worlds. Sin in this life and glory in the next!" But of course this is not gospel logic. Jude 4 warns of "ungodly people, who pervert the grace of our God into sensuality and deny our only Master and Lord, Jesus Christ."

Clearly, grace is no excuse for license. Paul loves to talk about the scandal of free grace. In fact, he never leaves that message behind. It's not like Paul hits grace hard for a while and then says, "Okay, enough about grace. Let's get down to business and talk about a whole lot of things you have to do now that you are justified." No, he never moves on from grace. But—and this is massively important—he was eager to extol the grace in justification *and* the grace in sanctification. Because of this grace, Paul says, and in the power of this grace, here's how you are going to be different now that you are a Christian.

Some people think all religions are the same. Every religion, they say, teaches you to love your neighbor, help the poor, deny yourself, and tell the truth. Well, even if it were true that all religions had basically the same ethics (and it most certainly isn't true), there would still be the issue of motivation. Why do these good things? Why be a "good" person? Is it to earn your way into heaven? Is it to support family values and Western civilization? Is it to get better karma? Is it to find enlightenment or rid yourself of cravings or achieve Nirvana? Is it to be released from the cycle of birth and rebirth? Or is being good important because it helps you feel better about yourself? The religions of the world don't agree on the rationale for our ethical behavior.

For Paul, the motivation starts (but doesn't end) with your identity in Christ. Look at Romans 6 and see what is objectively, definitively, irreversibly true of you as a Christian. You were baptized into Christ Jesus (v. 3). You were crucified with Christ (v. 6). You died with Christ (v. 8). You were buried with Christ (v. 4). You were raised with Christ (vv. 4, 5). When 1 Corinthians 10:2 says the Israelites "were baptized into Moses in the cloud and in the sea," it doesn't mean they were literally immersed in him or sprinkled with him. It means they were joined to him. They participated with Moses in the exodus—they as his people and he as their representative and head. In the same sense we are baptized into Christ. Whether our physical baptism takes places as an infant and is later appropriated by faith, or takes place as an adult with a profession of faith right then, we are meant to see in the sacrament a sign of our union with Christ.

As Christians we do not always feel close to Jesus. But that does not change the reality of our union with him. We are told to "*consider* [ourselves] dead to sin and alive to God in Christ Jesus" (Rom. 6:11) because that's what is true of us as Christians. We must reckon ourselves to be what we are in Jesus—dead to sin and alive to righteousness. I once heard a story about a man struggling with same-sex gender attraction who admitted to his mentor that he was going back to the gay bar scene that particular evening. His pastor simply told him, "I don't think you will, because that's not who you are." That's good counsel. And very biblical.

Union with Christ fundamentally and irrevocably changes our relationship to sin. Our old self has been crucified (Rom. 6:6), and sin has no dominion over us (v. 14). This doesn't mean a part of us called the "old nature" has been replaced with a different substance called a "new nature." Paul is not talking about *parts*. He is talking about *position*. The old man is what we were "in Adam" (cf. 5:12–21). Death, sin, punishment, transgression—that's the "in Adam" team. But we died to that team. The contract was revoked. We now wear the "in Christ" jersey. Union with Christ is like being placed on an NFL football team through no talent of your own. Though you didn't earn your way on to the team, now that you wear the jersey you want to play like a real football player.

Or, to use a few different analogies:

- Union with Christ is like being released from a nasty prison. You used to curl up in your bed when someone walked by because you didn't want to get beaten. You would pass dirty magazines through the wall. You would threaten and intimidate people to get first in line for the grub. But once you are out, you don't act like that anymore. You are in a different world now.
- Union with Christ is like a ten-year-old refusing to be called a "baby" by his friends. He knows he's not a baby anymore. He's a boy. So he starts acting more grown up.
- Union with Christ is like a student coming to college on a horse, unloading a quill and ink bottle, lighting a bunch of candles, and trying to communicate by Morse code, only to realize she's not in the right century. We'd all be surprised to meet such a college student. She needs to start living in the proper age.

Of course, these aren't perfect analogies. They don't take into account the way Christ also changes us from the inside out, but as imperfect examples they do get at Paul's argument in Romans 6.

Paul is not using union with Christ to play Jedi mind tricks on the church in Rome ("these aren't the sins you've been looking for"). Rather, he wants them to know and consider all that is true of them in Christ (Rom. 6:9, 11). Their identity, and yours, has been altered. You play for a different team. You live in a different age. You belong to a different realm. You go by a different name. *Therefore*, don't let sin reign in your mortal body (v. 12). Don't present your members to sin as instruments for unrighteousness (v. 13). Instead, offer yourselves to God as slaves to righteousness, leading to sanctification (v. 19).

The Bible is realistic about holiness. Don't think that all this glorious talk about dying to sin and living to God means there is no struggle anymore or that sin will never show up in the believer's life. The Christian life still entails obedience. It still involves a fight. But it's a fight we will win. You have the Spirit of Christ in your corner, rubbing your shoulders, holding the bucket, putting his arm around you and saying before the next round with sin, "You're going to knock him out, kid." Sin may get in some good jabs. It may clean your clock once in a while. It may bring you to your knees. But if you are in Christ it will never knock you out. You are no longer a slave, but free. Sin has no dominion over you. It can't. It won't. A new King sits on the throne. You serve a different Master. You salute a different Lord.

In effect God says to us, "Because you believe in Christ, by the Holy Spirit I have joined you to Christ. When he died, you died. When he rose, you rose. He's in heaven, so you're in heaven. He's holy, so you're holy. Your position right now, objectively and factually, is as a holy, beloved child of God, dead to sin, alive to righteousness, and seated in my holy heaven—now live like it." That's the way indicatives and imperatives work together in union with Christ. It's also the long way of saying "be who you are."

Chapter Eight

SAINTS AND SEXUAL IMMORALITY

I've tried hard in this book to avoid the sort of constant shaming that people expect when you talk about holiness. It is all too easy to blast people for not praying enough or not memorizing Scripture enough or not caring for the poor enough. Preachers can be quite adept at making every message about how you fall short of God's holiness. But I've written this book to make you hopeful about holiness, not make you hang your head.

And yet, when there is compromise with the world, we need conviction. We have to undergo the difficult task of looking at our lives and seeing how we may be out of step with Scripture. That's the goal of this chapter. The purpose, however, is not to push you down, but to lift you up into God's way, that you might follow God's will and live according to God's Word.

This chapter is about sexual immorality. You know that from the title. And you know from living in this world that sexual immorality is a huge problem. I don't have to convince you that we live in a culture flooded with sex. You can find it in stores, in songs, in sports, on billboards, on the beach, on the movie screen, on You Tube, on Hulu, on your iPhone, in the mall, in catalogs, in car magazines, and just about anywhere else you look. But this chapter is not about the culture *out there*. It's about those of us *here*—about what we as Christians are doing, what we are seeing, and what we may not know we are doing and seeing.

In the Old Testament, when a good king would take over in Israel or Judah he would rid the land of idols and false religion. And God would be pleased. But often, even with the good kings, we find that despite much progress "the high places were not taken away" (1 Kings 15:14; 22:43; 2 Kings 12:3; 14:4; 15:4, 35). These were the various sites in Israel where people would do sacrifices and rituals—the kinds that the other nations performed. The high places were a symbol of Israel's compromise. The high places were so entrenched in the culture, they seemed so normal, that even the good kings did not think to remove them. Or if they did, they couldn't muster the courage to act on their convictions. The high places were blind spots. The people couldn't see what they represented. They were so common, so ordinary, so much in keeping with the way things were, that the kings didn't tear them down and the people didn't stop worshiping there.

Sexual immorality is one of our high places. I'm afraid we—and there is an "I" in that "we"—don't have the eyes to see how much the world has squeezed us into its mold.

If we could transport Christians from almost any other century to any of today's "Christian" countries in the West, I believe what would surprise them most (besides our phenomenal affluence) is how at home Christians are with sexual impurity. It doesn't shock us. It doesn't upset us. It doesn't offend our consciences. In fact, unless it's really bad, sexual impurity seems normal, just a way of life, and often downright entertaining.

This is a far cry from how the Bible views sexual sin. If you go back to the vice lists, you'll see that every one of them mentions sexual immorality. More often than not when the apostle Paul lists behaviors not fitting for the Christian, sexual immorality is at the head of the list (Rom. 1:24; 1 Cor. 6:9; Gal. 5:19; Eph. 5:3; Col. 3:5). In moving from darkness to light, one of the first things new Gentile converts had to accept was a radically different sexual ethic.

So what does all this have to do with the previous chapter and union with Christ? Let's look at two passages in particular and see how God's standards for sexual purity may be higher than you think, and how the doctrine of union with Christ may be more helpful than you realize.

RUN, BABY, RUN!

We'll start with 1 Corinthians 6:12–20:

> [12] "All things are lawful for me," but not all things are helpful. "All things are lawful for me," but I will not be dominated by anything. [13] "Food is meant for the stomach and the stomach for food"—and God will destroy both one and the other. The body is not meant for sexual immorality, but for the Lord, and the Lord for the body. [14] And God raised the Lord and will also raise us up by his power. [15] Do you not know that your bodies are members of Christ? Shall I then take the members of Christ and make them members of a prostitute? Never! [16] Or do you not know that he who is joined to a prostitute becomes one body with her? For, as it is written, "The two will become one flesh." [17] But he who is joined to the Lord becomes one spirit with him. [18] Flee from sexual immorality. Every other sin a person commits is outside the body, but the sexually immoral person sins against his own body. [19] Or do you not know that your body is a temple of the Holy Spirit within you, whom you have from God? You are not your own, [20] for you were bought with a price. So glorify God in your body.

The big idea of this section is found in verse 18: flee from sexual immorality. Which begs the question, what exactly is sexual immorality? The word Paul uses is the usual word for sexual sin in the New Testament. It's the Greek word *porneia*. It refers to the broadest category of sexual sins and includes more than simply adultery (cf. Matt. 5:32, where Jesus uses *moicheia* for adultery and *porneia* for the larger category of sexual immorality). As one commentator observes, the term "can be found in Greek literature with reference to a variety of illicit sexual practices, including adultery, fornication, prostitution, and homosexuality. In the OT it occurs for any sexual practice outside marriage between a man and woman that is prohibited by the Torah."[1] Likewise, the leading Greek lexicon defines *porneia* as "unlawful sexual intercourse, prostitution, unchastity, fornication."[2]

The simplest way to understand *porneia* is to think about the things that would make you furious and heartbroken if you found out someone was doing them with your husband or your wife. If someone shook your wife's hand you would not be upset. If someone gave a casual side hug to your husband it probably wouldn't bother you. A kiss on the cheek or even a peck on the lips in some cultures might be appropriate. But if you found out another person had sex with your wife or saw her naked or touched certain parts of her body you would be furious. If you found another person made out with your husband or talked about sexual activities or made certain gestures you would be heartbroken. Why? Because these are all activities that are appropriate for a married couple but are inappropriate when practiced outside of the lawful relationship of a man and a woman in marriage. Any sexual activity between those who are not married, or between two men, or between two women, or among more than two persons, or between family members, or between those married to other people—any sexual activity in these contexts is sin and can be included in the

---

[1] James R. Edwards, *The Gospel according to Mark* (Grand Rapids, MI: Eerdmans, 2002), 213.
[2] Walter Bauer et al., *Greek-English Lexicon of the New Testament and Other Early Christian Literature*, 3rd ed. (Chicago: University of Chicago Press, 2000).

prohibitions against *porneia*. In simplest terms, sexual immorality, as Jesus and Paul and all the biblical writers understood it, is sexual activity outside of marriage between a man and a woman.

It's about all this that Paul says "flee." Don't reason with sexual sin, just run. Don't dabble. Don't peruse. Don't experiment. Don't "find yourself." Don't test your resolve. Don't mess around. Just flee. We are to avoid the mistakes of the foolish man in Proverbs 7 who hung around sexual immorality, listened to its siren song, followed it through town, and ended up losing his life. God doesn't ask us to get familiar with sexual immorality on the big screen, TV screen, or smart phone screen so that we can engage the culture. He commands us to get away.

MEMBERS OF CHRIST

In 1 Corinthians 6:12 we find Paul responding to one of the Corinthians' favorite slogans. Apparently they liked to affirm that "all things are lawful for me." They were proud of their Christian liberty. And yet Paul explains that even "free things" are not free if they enslave you. When examining gray areas in the Christian life, we need to do more than look for a specific Bible verse condemning the practice in question. We need to use bigger questions like the ones in verse 12. We need to ask, for example, whether masturbation is "helpful" to us in glorifying God (1 Cor. 10:31) or whether it enslaves us to habits we cannot break.

What is particularly instructive (and challenging and hopeful) about this section is Paul's emphasis on our identity with Christ. It's popular in our day to think our bodies belong to us: "No one can tell me what to do with *my* body!" In fact, in our culture nothing is more essential to our identity as human beings than the freedom to express ourselves sexually and use our bodies as we choose. But God says the body belongs to him, not to us. We are temples of the Holy Spirit (1 Cor. 6:19) and members of Christ (v. 15). The body is no longer for self-gratification, but for God-glorification (v. 20). We have been bought with a price and belong to Christ.

That may sound like bondage—"Now I have to do what God wants." And it is true that loving God means living by his commands. But belonging to Christ means freedom, not slavery. Don't think of Christianity as *having* to do what a peevish God wants. Think of it as now being *able* to do what a good God demands. Through union with Christ we are empowered for holiness. The same God who raised Jesus from the dead will raise us up to live for the Lord and not for the body (vv. 13–14). That's one of the gifts of being joined to Christ. Union with Christ means God's power for us working in and through us.

Union with Christ also means moral responsibility. Look at 1 Corinthians 6:15. Paul's language is circumspect, but his argument is quite shocking. Since we belong to Christ, we are members of his body. Therefore, when you engage in sexual immorality— whether it's prostitution, as Paul mentions, or adultery, or sex before marriage, or any other sexual sin—it's as if the members of Christ are engaging in sexual sin. To put it bluntly, if you shack up with a whore it's like dragging Christ into bed with her too. When you put your faith in Christ, you become one spirit with him (v. 17). So when you put your sexual organs where they don't belong, you are putting the Lord Jesus where he doesn't belong.

Sexual sin is terribly serious because it is a sin against your own body *and* a sin against the body of Christ of which you are a member. If you can't picture Christ with a prostitute or Christ in front of porn or Christ sleeping around, then you shouldn't picture yourself in those circumstances either. You belong to Christ. More than that, you are *joined* to Christ. If his body is pure, yours should be too.

HOLINESS IN A HOOKUP WORLD

Before moving on to our second passage, let's go back to this definition of *porneia* and try to apply it to a debated area of the Christian life: the dating relationship. I want to rush in where angels fear to tread and attempt to answer the age-old question "how far is too far?"

As I mentioned in chapter 3, my wife and I struggled with setting boundaries in our physical relationship when we were dating and later engaged. We sought advice from many Christians we respected and got a wide range of opinions—everything from "do nothing" to "try almost everything." Most often people basically said, "Don't have sex and set some boundaries, but what they are is between the two of you and the Lord."

We managed to set a host of boundaries. And break many of them too. Part of the problem was our self-control (mostly mine). But frankly, another part of the problem was even knowing what we were supposed to control, especially when we were in the strange limbo land of engagement. We knew sex was out of the question and so were a number of steps leading up to that. And yet, that left a lot of dangerous gray area within bounds. By God's grace we were both virgins when we got married. But I have to admit we didn't always keep to our own standards. And yet the issue went beyond that of a smitten conscience. Looking back, I don't think we kept to the Lord's standards either. As the man in the relationship and the one entirely to blame for pushing the envelope, I take responsibility for those sins. We've confessed them before the Lord long ago.

I share all that so young people reading this book know that I remember well what this struggle is like. I remember the confusion and the eagerness and the guilt. I am certainly not a model to follow in every respect. So what I am about to say may sound overly restrictive, especially coming from someone who is past the point of having to follow this advice. But I wish someone would have told me that it doesn't have to be so complicated. Maybe they tried and I didn't listen.

I know there is not an exact verse in Scripture that addresses the "how far is too far" question. If that verse existed, I guarantee you would have had a Bible study on it by now. You can't just turn to Hezekiah chapter 4 and find one verse to settle things. But the Bible tells us everything we need to know for life and godliness. There are principles to help us in this discussion.

First, the main goal in all relationships is to glorify God, not to get as close to sinning as possible. We aren't salvation minimalists interested in getting away with something. We want to know how to maximally please God before we are married.

Second, do not stir up love before its time (Song 2:7; 3:5; 8:4). These are powerful desires we are talking about and, in the wrong context, strong temptations. Many godly people have found themselves doing all sorts of things they never thought they'd be doing. You have a whole lifetime in front of you to figure things out, so be careful not to awaken passions that cannot yet be fulfilled. Better to err on the side of caution. I've never heard a Christian couple regret all they didn't do before they were married.

Third, and this is where things will seem radically counter-cultural to many believers, you should treat all the Christians you are not married to as your brothers and sisters in Christ. This is the argument Gerald Hiestand and Jay Thomas make in their helpful book *Sex, Dating, and Relationships.*[3] They argue that until we are married we should view members of the opposite sex against the backdrop of the family relationship. Indeed this was Paul's

---

[3]Gerald Hiestand and Jay S. Thomas, *Sex, Dating, and Relationships: A Fresh Approach* (Wheaton, IL: Crossway, 2012).

approach: "Do not rebuke an older man but encourage him as you would a father, younger men as brothers, older women as mothers, younger women as sisters, in all purity" (1 Tim. 5:1–2). So, young single men, what does purity look like toward your sister? Would you make out with her? Engage in passionate kissing? Be in bed together? By no means! She's your sister!! Well, there you have it: a standard for purity toward the spiritual sisters in your life. Unmarried Christians, the general rule is this: don't do with another guy or girl what you wouldn't do with your brother or sister.

What does this mean for "dating" then? For starters, I'm not against the word. I'm certainly not against single men taking the initiative with single women and pursuing them in an intentional, respectful way that points toward marriage. I'm all for that, and I don't get hung up on what we name it. Call it courtship or dating or intentional friendship. The label is not the important thing. What is important is to understand that the Bible has no category of dating where people who aren't married can kinda sorta start acting in some ways like they are. Hiestand and Thomas are right:

> Any and all sexual activity [outside of marriage], even when it stops short of more intense sexual expression, is outside the bounds of the Bible's sexual ethic. It is (can we say it so boldly?) a sin. And not only is such activity itself sinful; it inevitably leads to sexual and emotional frustration, which in turn leads to further sexual temptation. It's a perfect storm of presenting our "members as slaves to impurity and lawlessness leading to more lawlessness" (Rom. 6:19). This is a simple reality that no doubt many of you can testify to from your own experience, and one that we have seen played out over and over again in our respective churches among adolescents and single adults.[4]

---

[4]Ibid, 41.

Think about our definition of *porneia*. Sexual immorality is sexual activity outside of marriage between a man and a woman. It's the sort of thing you would be outraged to find your spouse or your parents doing with someone else. And yet, many Christians have no problem doing half of those same things with someone they are not married to. You wouldn't make out with a stranger. You wouldn't make out with your friend. But you would make out with someone you are dating. What's the difference? "Well, we are committed to each other," you say. But really you aren't. Dating couples can break up at any time—even during engagement in our culture—with no strings attached. The commitment in dating may be one of exclusivity but it is certainly not one of permanence. And without the promise or permanence it is hardly a commitment.

The bottom line is, you are not married until you are married. And until you are married, I believe it is a fair inference from biblical principles that you should refrain from all sexual activity—even the kind that stops well short of intercourse. Pursuing holiness in today's cheap-date, hookup world requires tremendous courage and other-worldliness. Long make-out sessions (and more) is not the way for young men to treat "younger women as sisters, in all purity" (1 Tim. 5:2). If you might not marry the one you are dating, why do all sorts of stuff with someone else's future spouse, stuff you will have a hard time forgetting once you are married yourself? And if you are on your way to marriage, instead of acting more married than single, consider getting married sooner so you don't have to act single any longer.

NOT EVEN A HINT

The second passage comes from Ephesians 5:3–12 and it is just as challenging as the first:

[3] But sexual immorality and all impurity or covetousness must not even be named among you, as is proper among saints. [4] Let there be no filthiness nor foolish talk nor crude joking, which are out of place, but instead let there be thanksgiving. [5] For you may be sure of this, that everyone who is sexually immoral or impure, or who is covetous (that is, an idolater), has no inheritance in the kingdom of Christ and God. [6] Let no one deceive you with empty words, for because of these things the wrath of God comes upon the sons of disobedience. [7] Therefore do not become partners with them; [8] for at one time you were darkness, but now you are light in the Lord. Walk as children of light [9] (for the fruit of light is found in all that is good and right and true), [10] and try to discern what is pleasing to the Lord. [11] Take no part in the unfruitful works of darkness, but instead expose them. [12] For it is shameful even to speak of the things that they do in secret.

Most basically, we see in this passage that sexual immorality is incompatible with the "kingdom" life (v. 5). People who give themselves over—unreservedly, unrepentantly—to sexual sin (and covetousness, for that matter) do not go to heaven. But notice, Paul doesn't stop at telling us to avoid *doing* these sins. God's Word gives a higher standard than that. Sexual immorality, impurity, covetousness (especially, in this context, the insatiable desire for someone else's body) is not even to be *named* among you. The NIV uses the phrase "not even a hint." Not too long ago I was driving in the car on my way to work, listening to a talk radio station. The host began talking about the latest "news" items concerning one of our trashier celebrities. As he laughed about this fresh revelation of moral turpitude, I found myself curious and disgusted at the same time. Thankfully I was working on this chapter at the time, so disgust won out and I turned the channel. "Not even a hint" does not allow for reveling in things that are scandalously unmentionable.

In the same manner, verse 4 speaks against filthiness, foolish talk, and crude joking. I remember, around about seventh grade, when certain boys in my class developed the ability to turn any remark into something sexual. If the teacher commented about chalk on the chalkboard, the back row of twelve-year-old boys giggled like a bunch of Tickle Me Stupids. It was so dumb, and I still have no idea what they were thinking. Some adult minds never grow out of such coarse joking. You can find it in the locker room or at the pub or on the youth retreat: dirty minds spilling out vulgar conversations with overtones and innuendo and double meanings.

These are challenging verses. What do they mean for the things we laugh about? What do they mean for the way we dress? What do these verses mean for the television we choose to watch or the movies we see for fun or the beer commercials interrupting every sporting event? Can we really justify all the innuendo, all the shameful secret things put out in broad daylight, all the sexual sin made to look normal, attractive, and amusing?

It's one thing to describe evil or even depict it. I'd never suggest that good writing or filmmaking must avoid the subject of sin. There are many thoughtful, tasteful movies, television shows, plays, musicals, and books out there—and the good ones usually deal with sin. Sin by itself is not the problem. The Bible is full of rank immorality. It would be simplistic and morally untenable—even unbiblical—to suggest you cannot watch sin or read about sin without sinning yourself. But the Bible never titillates with its description of sin. It never paints vice with virtue's colors. It does not entertain with evil (unless to mock it). The Bible does not dull the conscience by making sin look normal and righteousness look strange. And there are no pictures of plunging necklines.

We have to take a hard look at the things we choose to put in front of our faces. If there was a couple engaged in sexual activity on a couch in front of you, would you pull up a seat to watch? No, that would be perverse, voyeuristic. So why is it different when people record it first and then you watch? What if a good-looking guy or girl, barely dressed, came up to you on the beach and said, "Why don't you sit on your towel right here and stare at me for awhile?" Would you do it? No, that would be creepy. Why is it acceptable, then, when the same images are blown up the size of a three-story building?

If we're honest, we often seek exposure to sexual immorality and temptations to impurity and call it "innocent" relaxation. Commenting on Ephesians 5:3, Peter O'Brien observes that, as Christians, we should not only shun all forms of sexual immorality, we should "avoid thinking and talking about them."[5] Even our jesting should be pure, lest we show "a dirty mind expressing itself in vulgar conversation."[6] If, as O'Brien remarks, "talking and thinking about sexual sins 'creates an atmosphere in which they are tolerated and which can . . . promote their practice,'"[7] how can we justify paying money to see, taste, and laugh at sexual sin? How can we stare at sensuality which aims to amuse and arouse and weaken our conscience and deaden our sense of spiritual things (even if it is on ordinary cable or only rated PG-13)? We must consider the possibility that much of what churchgoing people do to unwind would not pass muster for the apostle Paul. Not to mention God.

I remember one night in seminary a bunch of us got together to watch the third Indiana Jones movie, the one about the Holy Grail. If you've seen it you may remember that, in this installment, Indiana

---

[5] Peter T. O'Brien, *The Letter to the Ephesians* (Grand Rapids, MI: Eerdmans, 1999), 360.
[6] Ibid., 361.
[7] Ibid., 360. O'Brien is quoting A.T. Lincoln here.

Jones (Harrison Ford) fights the bad guys with his father (Sean Connery). At one point in the film there is a surprising line from the senior Dr. Jones which reveals that he and his son had just slept with the same Nazi woman. It's meant to be a funny scene, and most of the seminarians in the room—both men and women—laughed out loud. But an older, respected student (not me!) called out the group. "Guys, they are talking about fornication and incest. It's really not funny." I think most of the people in the room were annoyed with such sermonizing. But the more I've thought about that incident over the years, the more I think the older man was right. A man and his father fornicating with the same woman? This kind of immorality was not tolerated even among the pagans in Paul's day (1 Cor. 5:1). He told the Corinthians to mourn over it (v. 2). But we laugh.

Brothers and sisters, we must be more vigilant. With our kids, with our families, with our Facebook accounts, with our texts, with our tweets, with our own eyes and hearts. Are we any different than the culture? Have we made a false peace with ourselves whereby we have said, we won't do the things you do or be as sensual as you are, but we will gladly watch you do them for us? The kinds of things Paul wouldn't even mention, the sort of sins he wouldn't dare joke about, the behaviors too shameful to even name—we hear about them in almost every sitcom and see them on screens bigger than our homes. Here is worldliness as much as anywhere in the Christian life. Try turning off the television and staying away from the movies for a month and see what new things you see when you come back. I fear many of us have become numb to the poison we are drinking. When it comes to sexual immorality, sin looks normal, righteousness looks very strange, and we look a lot like everybody else.

FIT FOR A KING

This is another area of sanctification where it pays to know our true identity in Christ. The contrast in Ephesians 5:3–12 is clear. The "sons of disobedience" and children of "darkness" meditate on and engage in sexual immorality. They walk in impurity because they are impure. By nature, children of darkness do shameful things in the dark. But as Christians, we are children of light. We belong to the kingdom of Christ and God. We are saints, holy ones declared holy in Christ, becoming holy by his Spirit. Sexual immorality isn't just wrong for us. It's not fitting. It's improper. At one time we may have been darkness, but now we are light in the Lord (v. 8). So why would we walk back into the shadows of sensuality, perversion, and senseless *porneia*? It's just not who we are.

I know it's easy to be overly dogmatic when talking about matters the Bible doesn't directly address, like movies and music, or dating and dress. We have to allow that good Christians will make different choices for themselves. I don't want to minimize the reality of Christian liberty and the role of the conscience. But if you are in Christ, please consider whether your conscience is functioning as well as it ought. The world is no friend to us in our fight for sexual purity. We daily inhale sexual air, are bombarded with sexual images, and are made to believe sexuality defines who we are. Sex sells, and even Christians who "wait" until marriage and confess their struggles to accountability partners are adept at buying the world's sexual wares through the Internet, at the ticket counter, in the mall, and by a thousand other means. Sexual immorality is everywhere to see, and too few of us with the mind of Christ are bothering to close our eyes.

A PASTORAL POSTSCRIPT

This chapter has been heavy on exhortation and light on comfort. That's intentional. I believe we are far too comfortable with sensuality and sexual sin. Many Christians need a wake-up call.

But I've also been a pastor long enough to know that some brothers and sisters reading this chapter already feel terrible about their sexual sin. They hate the pornography they love. They loathe the masturbation they can't escape. They regret all the things they've done and seen over the years. When it comes to sex, some Christians feel immediately dirty, rotten, and hopeless. If my words wound, it is only because my greater desire is to heal. No matter how entrenched the patterns of sin, I tell you on the authority of God's Word: your situation is not hopeless. With the gospel there is hope of cleansing. With the Spirit there is hope of power. With Christ there is hope of transformation. With the Word of God there is hope of holiness.

If you have died with Christ, will you not also be raised with Christ (Rom. 6:4–8)? If you have been crucified with Christ, is it not the person of Christ—with all his purifying power—who lives in you (Gal. 2:20)? And if God did not spare his own Son but gave him up for you, how will he not also with him graciously give you all things (Rom. 8:32)? God can forgive (again). God can empower (more). And God can change you, even if it's slowly, haltingly, and painfully from one itty-bitty degree of glory to the next.

Chapter Nine

ABIDE AND OBEY

We saw in chapter 3 that holiness is being *like* Christ. We saw in chapter 7 that being like Christ is possible only for those who are *in* Christ. Now I want to turn the sanctification diamond to another facet and argue that those in Christ should make it their aim to grow in fellowship *with* Christ. We must always remember that in seeking after holiness we are not so much seeking after a thing as we are seeking a person. The blessings of the gospel—election, justification, sanctification, glorification, and all the rest—have been deposited in no other treasury but Christ.[1] We don't just want holiness. We want the Holy One in whom we have been counted holy and are now being made holy. To run hard after holiness is another way of running hard after God. Just as a once-for-all, objective justification leads to a slow-growth, subjective sanctification, so our unchanging *union* with Christ leads to an ever-increasing *communion* with Christ.

---

[1]John Calvin writes, in one of the best paragraphs you'll ever read, "We see that our whole salvation and all its parts are comprehended in Christ [Acts 4:12]. We should therefore take care not to derive the least portion of it from anywhere else. If we seek salvation we are taught by the very name of Jesus that it is 'of him' [1 Cor. 1:30]. If we seek any other gifts of the Spirit, they will be found in his anointing. If we seek strength, it lies in his dominion; if purity, in his conception; if gentleness, it appears in his birth. For by his birth he was made like us in all respects [Heb. 2:17] that he might learn to feel our pain [cf. Heb. 5:2]. If we seek redemption, it lies in his passion; if acquittal, in his condemnation; if remission of the curse, in his cross [Gal. 3:13]; if satisfaction, in his sacrifice; if purification, in his blood; if reconciliation, in his descent into hell; if mortification of the flesh, in his tomb; if newness of life, in his resurrection; if immortality, in the same; if inheritance of the Heavenly Kingdom, in his entrance into heaven; if protection, if security, if abundant supply of all blessings, in his Kingdom; if untroubled expectation of judgment, in the power given to him to judge. In short, since rich store of every kind of good abounds in him, let us drink our fill from this fountain and from no other" (*Institutes* 2.16.19).

UNION AND COMMUNION

Several years ago our church adopted a new statement of faith. In one of the articles we talked about "union" and "communion" with Christ. An astute member asked if those two words weren't redundant—don't "union" and "communion" really say the same thing? True, they are related; but they are not synonymous. *Union with Christ* is the irrevocable work of the Spirit. Once united, nothing can separate us from Christ. Nothing can make us a little more or a little less united. Union with Christ is unalterable. *Communion with Christ*, on the other hand, can be affected by sin and unresponsiveness to God's grace. It's like marriage: you can't be more or less married (union) but you can have a stronger or weaker marriage (communion).Our relationship with Christ can also deepen when we attend to the divinely appointed means of grace. Or to put it somewhat paradoxically, we who enjoy saving fellowship *in* Christ ought to cultivate a growing fellowship *with* Christ. As Calvin says, "Not only does [Christ] cleave to us by an indivisible bond of fellowship, but with a wonderful communion, day by day, he grows more and more into one body with us, until he becomes completely one with us."[2]

I don't want to belabor the point, but it's important we understand that communion with Christ is predicated on union with Christ and not the other way around. Some mystical and contemplative traditions emphasize communion with Christ without paying sufficient attention to how we are first joined to Christ by faith. The call of the gospel does not begin with an invitation to meditate on Christ or lose oneself in God. The gospel announces the person and work of Christ and then calls us to trust in his person

---

[2]*Institutes* 3.2.24.

and work. As Sinclair Ferguson points out, "Contemplation is not the way of salvation; atonement is."[3] We cannot bypass the central apostolic categories of incarnation, redemption, substitution, propitiation, reconciliation, and justification and go straight to communion with God. The summons of the gospel is not to meditate or contemplate, but to repent and believe. Only through this exercise of faith can we have union with Christ. And then from this union it is our privilege and responsibility to pursue deeper communion with Christ.

By communion I simply mean fellowship with Christ. In his brilliant work *Communion with God* (1657), John Owen takes four hundred pages to unpack how we can have communion with each distinct member of the Trinity. The Father's special communion with us is love; the Son's communion is grace; and the Spirit's communion with us is comfort. The book demonstrates at length that "communion" is an all-encompassing and complicated theme. But thankfully, behind all of Owen's dense prose is the central and rather simple thesis that communion with God consists of "mutual relations" between God and us.[4] So when I speak of communion with Christ I mean strengthening our relationship with him. As our communion deepens, we enjoy sweeter fellowship and interchange with him. We grow in knowledge of him and affection for him, and we experience more richly his love and affection for us. And most crucially (for our purposes), as we deepen our communion with Christ—seeing and savoring his grace more and more each day—we also obey Christ more fully and more freely.

[3]Sinclair Ferguson, "The Reformed View," in *Christian Spirituality: Five Views of Sanctification*, ed. Donald L. Alexander (Downers Grove, IL: IVP Academic, 1988), 195.

[4]Kelly M. Kapic, "Worshiping the Triune God: The Shape of John Owen's Trinitarian Spirituality," in *Communion with the Triune God*, ed. Kelly M. Kapic and Justin Taylor (Wheaton, IL: Crossway, 2007), 20.

KEEPING COMMANDMENTS, ABIDING IN LOVE

It's tempting to see communion with Christ and the pursuit of holiness as opposite approaches to the Christian life. You can just imagine one group of Christians insisting on a personal relationship with Jesus and another group saying, "No, no, it's all about obeying Jesus." One group claims the other is legalistic, while that bunch of Christians says the first group is too caught up in subjective mumbo-jumbo.

But the Bible allows for no such division between communion with Christ and obedience to Christ. In fact, it's very hard to tell the two apart. In John 15, Jesus tells the disciples, "Abide in me, and I in you" (John 15:4). "I am the vine," Jesus says, "you are the branches. Whoever abides in me and I in him, he it is that bears much fruit, for apart from me you can do nothing" (v. 5). Christ abides in us, and we must abide in him. But how do we abide in Christ? Verses 9–11 explain that we abide in him by obeying him. If we obey Christ's commandments, we will abide in his love (v. 10). This mutual indwelling—Christ in us and we in Christ—cannot be separated from personal holiness. D. A. Carson puts it well: "God remains among us and in his people by renewing them with his life, with his Spirit, and making his presence known in them and among them (*cf.* 14:16, 23); they remain in him by obeying his commands."[5]

Of course, we must be careful not to impose a strict temporal order between abiding and obeying. If we do, we'll make the mistake of thinking that we need to obey before we can abide. Or just as bad, we'll tie ourselves up in knots trying to abide with all our heart before we get around to obedience. The reality is the two are

---

[5] D. A. Carson, *The Gospel According to John* (Grand Rapids, MI: Eerdmans, 1991), 516–517.

virtually synonymous. We obey as we abide and abide as we obey. Frustrated believers need to be reminded that they will bear fruit only as they are connected to the Vine. Apart from Jesus they can do nothing (vv. 5–6). Likewise, lazy believers need to be reminded that if they are serious about remaining in Christ's love and experiencing abundant life they must get serious about obeying the Father's commandments (vv. 10–11). Fellowship with Christ does not exist apart from fealty to Christ.

We see this connection just as clearly in John's epistles as we do in his Gospel. If we abide in Christ we must walk in the same way he walked (1 John 2:6). No one who abides in Christ keeps on sinning (3:6). Whoever does not love does not have eternal life abiding in him (3:15). Whoever keeps the commandments abides in God and God in him (3:24). If we love one another, God abides in us and we abide in God (4:12, 16). As we've already seen, John is not telling us to be morally flawless. There is an Advocate we can fly to for forgiveness (1:9; 2:1). But finding assurance in Christ is no excuse for presumption when our lives are marked by apathetic (or defiant!) disobedience to Christ. The verb "to abide" occurs more in John's writings than in all the rest of the New Testament combined. He wants us to see that fellowship with Christ is wonderfully possible in this life and in the next. But this fellowship must be given practical proof.[6] A complete disregard for holiness indicates that we do not have fellowship with Christ and are not in him. Conversely, walking with Christ and enjoying communion with him involves walking as Christ did and keeping his commands.

---

[6] See Rudolf Schnackenburg, *The Johannine Epistles: A Commentary* (New York: Crossroad, 1992), 103.

FOUR PRACTICES FOR ONENESS WITH CHRIST

If communion with Christ is essential for holiness, must result in holiness, and sometimes seems to be virtually identical to holiness, we would do well to consider how we can deepen that communion. Or to put it another way, if union with Christ means it is our privilege and responsibility to pursue communion with Christ, what do we actually do to enrich and enjoy this communion?

Part of the answer is nothing. We don't do anything. But God does a lot of things to us, with us, and through us. Our feelings go up and down. Our sense of closeness fluctuates. But God is always there. He has a way of sanctifying us apart from our conscious effort. He quietly brings events and conditions into our lives that humble us, purify us, and draw us to Christ. Quite often, God uses suffering to smooth out our rough edges and break down our streak of independence. We may not be aware of any particular patterns that have led us to Christ, but over the years we may find that indeed our love for Jesus is stronger, our relationship with him is firmer, and our sense of his presence is stronger. Even in the dark times and dry seasons, we will find that God has been working all along. In thinking about our fellowship with Christ we must never imagine that Christ is hiding in a corner, waiting for us to break through his hard exterior, just hoping we'll pay attention to him. He is constantly reaching out, wooing, speaking, entreating, moving, and standing at the door to knock (Rev. 3:20).

If part of the answer is nothing, then another part of the answer must be something. True, Christ works, often imperceptibly, without our knowing participation, to draw us closer to himself. But we also have a role to play. Just as in any relationship, there are practices we must develop and work hard at if we are to grow in our communion with Christ.

(1) *We pursue communion with Christ through prayer.* It's easy to demonstrate from the Bible that we must pray. Jesus made it a priority to pray (Mark 1:35). He taught his disciples how to pray (Matt. 6:5–13). We are commanded to "continue steadfastly in prayer" (Col. 4:2) and even to "pray without ceasing" (1 Thess. 5:17). If there is one thing Christians all agree on, it's that God wants us to pray.

And if there is another thing Christians all agree on, it's that we feel guilty about not praying more. I doubt there has ever been a Christian who got to the end of his life and thought, "You know what, I'm glad I didn't spend more time in prayer." We all know we should pray and we all want to pray—or at least we want to want to. But we all know from experience that "ought to" is not enough to get us to pray consistently. What's missing is this element of communion. It's not enough to screw up our resolve, set the alarm fifteen minutes earlier, and mumble through a few more minutes of prayer so that we can feel good about our spiritual disciplines. We need to understand that time spent in prayer is time spent with our Maker, Defender, Redeemer, and Friend. Communion is the goal, not crossing off a line on our to-do list.

Consider two different exhortations to prayer. The first is from William Law (1686–1781) in *A Serious Call to a Devout and Holy Life*:

> I take it for granted, that every Christian, that is in health, is up early in the morning; for it is much more reasonable to suppose a person up early, because he is a Christian, than because he is a labourer, or a tradesman, or a servant, or has business that wants him. . . .

Let this therefore teach us to conceive how odious we must appear in the sight of Heaven, if we are in bed, shut up in sleep and darkness, when we should be praising God; and are such slaves to drowsiness, as to neglect our devotions for it.

For if he is to be blamed as a slothful drone, that rather chooses the lazy indulgence of sleep, than to perform his proper share of worldly business; how much more is he to be reproached, that would rather lie folded up in bed, than be raising up his heart to God in acts of praise and adoration! . . .

Sleep is such a dull, stupid state of existence, that even amongst mere animals, we despise them most which are most drowsy.

He, therefore, that chooses to enlarge the slothful indulgence of sleep, rather than be early at his devotions to God, chooses the dullest refreshment of the body; before the highest, noblest employment of the soul; he chooses that state which is a reproach to mere animals, rather than exercise which is the glory of Angels.[7]

That's one way to entice the believer to pray. Here's another, this time from Thomas Goodwin (1600–1680):

Mutual communion is the soul of all true friendship; and a familiar converse with a friend hath the greatest sweetness in it . . . (so) besides the common tribute of daily worship you owe to (God), take occasion to come into his presence on purpose to have communion with him. This is truly friendly, for friendship is most maintained and kept up by visits; and these, the more free and less occasioned by urgent business, or solemnity . . . the more friendly they are . . . We used to check our friends with this upbraiding. "You still (always) come when you have some business, but when will you come to *see me*?" . . . When thou comest into his presence, be telling him still how well thou lovest him; labour to abound in expressions of that kind, than which . . . there is nothing more taking with the heart of any friend.[8]

Which approach will serve you better over the long haul?

[7]William Law, *A Serious Call to a Devout and Holy Life* (ReadaClassic, 2010), 141–142.
[8]Quoted by J. I. Packer, "The Puritan Idea of Communion with God," in *Puritan Papers, Volume 2 1960–1962* (Phillipsburg, NJ: P&R, 2001), 114–115 (emphasis his).

William Law makes me deathly afraid of the snooze bar. Thomas Goodwin makes me want to pray. Who wouldn't want the happiness of drawing near to God? Who doesn't delight to tell secrets and converse with a friend? Prayer (this side of heaven) will always be hard and will always take discipline, but when I see it as a means to communion with God, it feels more like a "get to" than a "have to."

(2) *We pursue communion with Christ through the word of truth.* Earlier we saw from John 15 that abiding in Christ entails obedience to Christ. In the same passage Jesus also connects his *words* with abiding. "If you abide in me, and my words abide in you, ask whatever you wish, and it will be done for you" (John 15:7). Notice how Christ's words are synonymous with his person. We take hold of Christ as his words take hold of us. Mutual indwelling involves more than just obedience. It also "entails a growing absorption of Jesus' teaching" into our heads and hearts.[9]

It's unfortunate that some church leaders and scholars like to shame Christians for making too much of the Bible. "We worship Jesus, not words on a page" is how the barb usually goes. Well, of course, we don't bow down before ink and paper. But don't think for a second that making much of the Bible is somehow antithetical to heartfelt communion with Christ. One of the recurring themes in 1 John is that we abide in Christ by letting the apostolic deposit of truth abide in us. It is only when we confess that Jesus is the Son of God, that God abides in us (1 John 4:15). If we do not have the truth about the Son, we do not have life (2:23; 5:12). Those who truly belong to God listen to his inspired, apostolic messengers (4:6). Doctrine is not a distraction from Christ. In fact,

---

[9] Andreas J. Köstenberger, *John* (Grand Rapids, MI: Baker Academic, 2004), 455.

we do not have communion with Christ apart from truth about Christ and from Christ. We are sanctified in the truth, and God's Word is truth (John 17:17).

(3) *We pursue communion with Christ through fellowship with other Christians.* Because the church is the body of Christ, we cannot have communion with Christ without also communing with our fellow Christians. Fellowship within the family of God is one expression of communion with Christ. John says, "that which we have seen and heard we proclaim also to you, so that you too may have fellowship with us; and indeed our fellowship is with the Father and with his Son Jesus Christ" (1 John 1:3). That's a remarkable statement. No matter how goofy or insignificant your church may seem, fellowship in that body of believers is fellowship with God.[10] Those serious about communing with Christ will be diligent to share in fellowship with other Christians (Acts 2:42; Heb. 10:24–25). In more than a decade of pastoral ministry I've never met a Christian who was healthier, more mature, and more active in ministry by being apart from the church. But I have found the opposite to be invariably true. The weakest Christians are those least connected to the body. And the less involved you are, the more disconnected those following you will be. The man who attempts Christianity without the church shoots himself in the foot, shoots his children in the leg, and shoots his grandchildren in the heart.

---

[10]John Owen begins his massive work *Communion with the Triune God* (89–90) by referencing 1 John 1:3: "The outward appearance and condition of the saints in those days being very mean and contemptible—their leaders being accounted as the filth of this world and as the offscouring of all things—the inviting [of] others into fellowship with them and a participation of the precious things which they did enjoy, seem to be exposed to many contrary reasonings and objections: 'What benefit is there in *communion* with them? Is it anything else but to be sharers in troubles, reproaches, scorns, and all manner of evils?' To prevent or remove these and the like exceptions, the apostle gives them to whom he wrote to know . . . that notwithstanding all the disadvantages their fellowship lay under, unto a carnal view, yet in truth it was, and would be found to be . . . very honorable, glorious, and desirable. For 'truly,' says he, 'our fellowship is with the Father and with his Son Jesus Christ.'"

(4) *We pursue communion with Christ through partaking of the Lord's Supper.* It's not surprising that in thinking about communion with Christ I would talk about prayer and the Word and fellowship. These are basic expectations of the Christian life. But some of you may be surprised, even concerned, that I would put the Lord's Supper on the list. You shouldn't be. After all, don't we regularly refer to this sacrament or ordinance as "communion"? Paul said "the cup of blessing that we bless" is "a participation in the blood of Christ" and "the bread that we break" is "a participation in the body of Christ" (1 Cor. 10:16). The word "participation" (or "communion" in the KJV) is a Greek word you may be familiar with: *koinonia*. According to the Bible, when you come to the Lord's Table in faith, you have *koinonia* with Christ. You fellowship with him and participate in his body and blood.

The Lord's Supper is not only a visible reminder of the gospel, it is a spiritual feast where Christ is present as both the host and the meal. His presence is not physical, but it is real. At the Table, Christ nourishes us, strengthens us, and assures us of his love. We do not celebrate an absent Christ in the Supper, but enjoy communion with the living Christ. As Richard Baxter remarked, "No where is God so near to man as in Jesus Christ; and no where is Christ so familiarly represented to us, as in this holy sacrament."[11]

EXTRAORDINARY HOLINESS THROUGH ORDINARY MEANS

If we're honest, communion with God is not a priority for many of us. At best, it sounds unrealistic. At worst, it sounds irrelevant. Communion with God is a small thing to us. We do not

---

[11]Quoted by Packer, "Puritan Idea of Communion with God," 116.

marvel that we can have fellowship with God in the first place. If anything, we take it for granted. We figure God is with everyone and has every reason to enjoy being with us. But neither assertion is true. God may be everywhere, but he is only *with*—in a covenantal sense—those who believe in his Son. Communion with God is possible only because of union with Christ. And what a remarkable possibility! The goal in the Garden was uninterrupted fellowship with God. The aim ever since has been restored fellowship with God. The end of the story is eternal fellowship with God. As J. I. Packer says, communion between God and man "is the end to which both creation and redemption are the means; it is the goal to which both theology and preaching must ever point; it is the essence of true religion; it is, indeed, the definition of Christianity."[12] That sinners can have fellowship with a sinless God is astonishing. That God made his Son who had no sin to be sin for us so that we could be reconciled to God is more amazing still (2 Cor. 5:21). And that we, with unveiled faces, can look upon the glory of God in the face of Christ and be transformed from one degree of glory to the next is yet one more undeserved blessing (3:18). You can know God. You can commune with God. You can be holier than you think.

And the process is more mundane than you might have imagined. If you are thoroughly underwhelmed with my four points for pursuing communion with Christ, I don't apologize. It may sound boring or out-of-date, but it just happens to be true: the way to grow in your relationship with Jesus is to pray, read your Bible, and go to a church where you'll get good preaching, good fellowship, and receive the sacraments. I'm not suggesting Christianity can be boiled down to a few external requirements. I'm not saying that at

---

[12]Ibid., 104. See also p. 105 for Packer's indictment of contemporary Christianity for making too little out of communion with God. My thoughts here are indebted to his.

all. I'm arguing that if you want to be Christlike you need to have communion with Christ, and if you want communion with Christ you need to do it on his terms with the channels of grace he's provided. And that means the only way to extraordinary holiness is through ordinary means.

Chapter Ten

THAT ALL MAY SEE YOUR PROGRESS

It was several years ago, not long after my ordination, that I stumbled upon 1 Timothy 4:15 and found it to be a source of both great comfort and mild discouragement. It wasn't the first time I had read the verse. But it was the first time God opened my eyes to the verse to see what it meant for my life and ministry.

Most pastors are familiar with 1 Timothy 4:16—"Keep a close watch on yourself and on the teaching." That's our blueprint for ministry: watch our lives and watch our doctrine. I knew verse 16 but hadn't paid much attention to verse 15: "Practice these things, immerse yourself in them, so that all may see your progress." It was that last part about progress that caught my eye. Earlier, in 1 Timothy 3, Paul lays out what seem like lofty requirements for elders and deacons. Then in 1 Timothy 4, just a few verses earlier, he tells young Timothy to "set the believers an example in speech, in conduct, in love, in faith, in purity" (v. 12). Does that feel a little intense to you? "Hey, Timmy, I know you are just out of seminary but I want you to be exemplary in pretty much every area of your life. Got it?" Sounds scary. But then comes this part about progress in verse 15. Apparently, Paul didn't think "set an example" meant "get everything right the first time."

You can take verse 15 as an upper or a downer. My discouragement came in thinking that people would see me five years from now and realize I used to be less mature, less capable, and less godly. It's a little bit of a bummer to realize that later I'll look back at the me I am now and be glad I'm not entirely the same me any longer. But verse 15 has mainly been an encouragement. It means I can be qualified to be an elder and set an example with my life without "having arrived." I can grow. I can mature. I can become holier than I am now. My behavior and my teaching can improve. Progress is not only what God expects from me but what he *allows* from me.

Which brings us to one of the most important axioms about holiness: when it comes to sanctification, it's more important where you're going than where you are. Direction matters more than position. Your future progress speaks louder than your present placement. So cheer up: if you aren't as holy as you want to be now, God may still be pleased with you because you are heading in the right direction. And be warned: if you aren't as holy as you used to be, God probably isn't impressed with yesterday's triumphs when for the last few months you've done nothing but give up.

I should hasten to add that measuring your progress in the pursuit of holiness is easier said than done. For starters, you shouldn't take your spiritual temperature every day. You need to look for progress over months and years, not by minutes and hours. As David Powlison likes to say, sanctification is like a man walking up the stairs with a yo-yo. There are a lot of ups and downs, but ultimate progress nonetheless. So don't tie yourself up in knots wondering if Tuesday was godlier than Wednesday. Look at your trajectory over the last five months, or better yet, over the last five years. This goes for judging others too. Don't rush to criticize the spiritual progress of others without knowing how far they've come and in which direction they're heading.

Which leads to a related point: don't be afraid to hand the spiritual thermometer over to someone else. The assumption in verse 15 is that *other Christians* will notice our progress. An honest, discerning friend is often more accurate than we are in assessing our relative spiritual health. They can see your general movement while you may only see today's failure. Remember, it's the testimony of almost all saints that as they get closer to God they see more of their ungodliness. It's normal to feel less holy as you become more holy. Being more aware of sin in your life is usually a sign of the Spirit's sanctifying work, not of his withdrawal. All that to say, when it comes to seeing your own sanctification, it's not always best to take your own word for it. Ask your wife, ask your roommate, ask your dad, ask your pastor, ask your best friend: can you see my progress?

REPENTANCE AS A WAY OF LIFE

If the pursuit of holiness entails progress—with fits and starts, with victories and defeats, with two steps forward and one step back—then it also demands repentance. In the very first of Martin Luther's 95 Theses he said, "Our Lord and Master Jesus Christ. . . . willed that the whole life of believers should be repentance." Sanctification, therefore, will be marked by penitence more than perfection. Of course, perfection does not have to be a bad word. The Greek word sometimes translated as "perfect" (*teleios* or *teleioō*) simply means qualified, mature, or fulfilled (Col. 1:28; 4:12; Heb. 2:10; James 1:4). So in one sense believers are to be "perfect." But biblically this never means complete sinlessness in thought or deed. Whatever you make of Romans 7 (and I think Paul is writing about his own struggle with sin as a Christian), it's undeniable that even the best believers sometimes do things they don't want to do and fail to do what they want to do. The Bible is clear—except for Jesus, no one will be sinless in this life (Heb. 4:15). "There is no one who does not sin" (1 Kings 8:46). There is "not a righteous man on earth who does good and never sins" (Eccles. 7:20). "If we say we have no sin, we deceive ourselves, and the truth is not in us" (1 John 1:8). Given these stark realities, holiness on earth must include repentance.

This is especially true because those most eager to be holy are often most susceptible to judgmentalism and arrogance. Everyone in love with the idea of personal holiness (not to mention those audacious enough to write a book on it!) should pay attention to the words of Andrew Murray: "There is no pride so dangerous, none so subtle and insidious, as the pride of holiness."[1] It's not that they would ever say it out loud, but there grows up in some Christians a sense of superiority concerning how far they have advanced compared to others. It is very possible to pursue holiness out of pride. It is also possible to pursue holiness out of humility, and succeed, and then become proud. It's not for nothing that Jesus expects his followers to ask for forgiveness as a regular part of their prayers (Matt. 6:12). Repentance is a way of life for the holy child of God.

Wrapping up a book on holiness with a section on repentance may seem counterintuitive. A little weak and a little defeatist. Kind of like telling a recovering alcoholic what to take for his next hangover. But if repentance looks like a concession to sin rather than a mark of holiness it's only because we think of repentance too lightly. It's one thing to sin your heart out, mumble a few sorrys, and get on with life. It's quite another thing to hate your sin, cry out to God, and make a spiritual U-turn. Real contrition is hard, painful work. As Thomas Brooks put it, quite vividly, "Repentance

---

[1] Andrew Murray, *Humility* (New Kensington, PA: Whitaker, 1982), 56.

is the vomit of the soul."[2] Think about throwing up for a moment (just a moment!). There is nothing pleasant about it. I can't think of any physical sensation I like less. I don't use puking as a backup plan, as a remedy I can always rely on later. When I throw up it tells me I have the flu, a migraine, or I ate too much at Taco John's. Something is terribly wrong.

Genuine repentance is similar. It's not a convenient escape hatch after a weekend or a life of folly. It means admitting specific wrong, recognizing your offensiveness to God, changing course, turning to Christ, and wishing with all your heart you had never made the mistake you now despise. Or as Calvin put it, "[repentance] is the true turning of our life to God, a turning that arises from a pure and earnest fear of him; and it consists in the mortification of our flesh and of the old man, and in the vivification of the Spirit."[3] Throwing up is not easy. And neither is repentance. But one is much sweeter than the other.

WHAT KIND OF GRIEF?

If we are going to understand the nature of true repentance, we need to be familiar with Paul's distinction in 2 Corinthians 7:9–11 between worldly grief and godly grief:

> [9] As it is, I rejoice, not because you were grieved, but because you were grieved into repenting. For you felt a godly grief, so that you suffered no loss through us.
> [10] For godly grief produces a repentance that leads to salvation without regret, whereas worldly grief produces death. [11] For see what earnestness this godly grief has produced in you, but also what eagerness to clear yourselves, what indignation, what fear, what longing, what zeal, what punishment! At every point you have proved yourselves innocent in the matter.

---

[2]Thomas Brooks, *Precious Remedies against Satan's Devices* (Edinburgh: Banner of Truth, 1997 [1652]), 63.
[3]*Institutes* 3.3.5.

I'm convinced all of us feel grief. Even the non-Christians I talk to are quick to acknowledge they're not perfect. People may not think they're bad enough to deserve God's wrath, but they know they've made mistakes. They feel regret for some things in their lives. That's grief. But not all grief is the same. Some grief is worldly. Most of us assume that feeling sorry for something is morally neutral. There isn't a right and wrong way to feel bad; you just feel it. In fact, if anything, we consider grief over some action we've taken to be an automatic good. "I may have screwed up royally, but now I feel really rotten about the whole thing." At least I regret my actions, we figure.

But according to the Bible, it is possible to feel sorry in a worldly way. Worldly grief is an expression of regret over opportunities lost, painful present circumstances, or personal embarrassment. We regret getting drunk on the weekend and blowing the test on Monday. We are sorry for having gambled away $10,000 at the casino. We feel terrible that our unflattering email got forwarded to the wrong person. Though we feel bad in all three situations, the regret may not have any spiritual dimension to it. We may just regret getting caught, hurting ourselves, or looking stupid.

Worldly grief is not good grief; it leads to death (2 Cor. 7:10). Because worldly grief does not allow us to see our offensiveness to God, we don't deal with our sin in a vertical direction. And when we don't repent upward, we don't get forgiveness from God, the lack of which leads to spiritual death. Worldly grief deals with symptoms, not with the disease. It produces despair, bitterness, and depression because it focuses on regret for the past (which can't be changed) instead of personal sinfulness (which can always be forgiven).

Ironically, if you say "I can't forgive myself," it's probably a sign of worldly grief—either unbelief in God's promises and the sufficiency of Christ's work on the cross, or regret that is merely focused on your loss of esteem and your loss of opportunities.

Godly grief is different. To use the words of the Heidelberg Catechism, godly grief "is to be genuinely sorry for sin, to hate it more and more, and to run away from it" (Q/A 89). The prodigal son saw that he not only had made a mess of his life, but he had sinned against his father, the one who loved him the most and had given him everything. This is exemplary. Too often we are simply sorry we got caught. Sorry we have to live with the consequences. Sorry we got knocked down a few notches in some people's estimation. Godly grief doesn't blame parents or the schools or the government or friends or the church. Godly grief says, "Have mercy on me, O God, according to your steadfast love; according to your abundant mercy blot out my transgressions. Wash me thoroughly from my iniquity, and cleanse me from my sin!" (Ps. 51:1–2).

Godly grief recognizes the utter sinfulness of sin and hates it more and more. The Corinthians were indignant that they had been implicated in this attack on the apostle Paul (2 Cor. 7:11). They wanted to clear their names and make things right. They were zealously opposed to their own mistakes. Their grief led to repentance (v. 9)—which means that feeling bad for something is not the same as repentance, but it can get you there.

There is an eternal difference between regret and repentance. Regret feels bad about past sins. Repentance turns away from past sins. Regret looks to our own circumstances. Repentance looks to God. Most of us are content with regret. We just want to feel bad for awhile, have a good cry, enjoy the cathartic experience, bewail our sin, and talk about how sorry we are. But we don't want to change. We don't want to deal with God. Godly grief is a fruitful and effective emotion. The Spirit uses it to spur us to action, to make us zealous for good works, and to help us run from sin and start walking in the opposite direction. Worldly grief makes you idle and stagnant. It leads you to wallow in self-pity and pointless regret. You don't change. You don't grow. You don't fight against the deeds of the flesh. Instead you just ruminate on your mistakes, obsess over the opinions of others, and ponder what might have been. Anyone can feel bad. Being changed is something else entirely. Sincere biblical repentance is as much a work of grace as not sinning in the first place. To err is human, to make progress is divine.

GROWING INTO A GOOD-LOOKING CHRISTIAN

Back when I was in college I had a conversation with an older Christian man about my plans to enter the ministry. In the course of our conversation he quoted a line that I've never forgotten. It comes from Robert Murray M'Cheyne, a nineteenth-century Scottish preacher who died at the age of twenty-nine. In fact, of all the sentences outside the Bible, I've probably repeated this one more than any other: "the greatest need of my people is my own holiness." Now in one sense, I suppose the gospel is more important than holiness, because the good news of Christ's death and resurrection is good even if the person sharing it is a scoundrel. So maybe M'Cheyne should have said, "the second greatest need." But in either case, he's absolutely right about the importance of holiness. He understood the indispensable character of character. We think relevance and relate-ability are the secrets to spiritual success. And yet, in truth, a dying world needs you to be with God more than it needs you to be "with it." That's true for me as a pastor and true for you as a mother, father, brother, sister, child, grandparent, friend, Bible study leader, computer programmer, bank teller, barista, or CEO. Your friends and family, your col-

leagues and kids—they don't need you to do miracles or trans-
form civilization. They need you to be holy. As Horatius Bonar
(another Scottish preacher and a friend of M'Cheyne) reminds us,
holiness is not measured by "one great heroic act or mighty mar-
tyrdom. . . . It is of small things that a great life is made up."[4]

Holiness is the sum of a million little things—the avoidance
of little evils and little foibles, the setting aside of little bits of
worldliness and little acts of compromise, the putting to death of
little inconsistencies and little indiscretions, the attention to little
duties and little dealings, the hard work of little self-denials and
little self-restraints, the cultivation of little benevolences and little
forbearances. Are you trustworthy? Are you kind? Are you patient?
Are you joyful? Do you love? These qualities, worked out in all the
little things of life, determine whether you are blight or blessing to
everyone around you, whether you are an ugly spiritual eyesore or
growing up into a good-looking Christian.

We live in a world obsessed with superficial beauty. Whether
it's on cable news or on the Weather Channel, the world expects a
certain look. The message all around us is that you're not good if
you're not good-looking. And so all of us—from ten-year-olds in
makeup, to college students in ironic hipster garb, to stay-at-home
moms on another diet, to middle-aged dads getting reacquainted
with the gym, to aging boomers on Botox—we're all interested in
beauty. But what is true beauty? What is really worth seeing? Who
has the look really worth imitating? Paul says, "Brothers, join in
imitating me, and keep your eyes on those who walk according to
the example you have in us" (Phil. 3:17). It's godliness that God is
looking for. The best-looking Christian is the one growing by the
Spirit into the likeness of Christ. It's all too common to think of

---

[4]Horatius Bonar, *God's Way of Holiness* (Lexington, KY: Legacy Publications), 82–83. My next
paragraph is a further summary of Bonar's description of holiness in the "small things."

holiness as some sort of snooty do-goodism, prudish moralism, or ugly legalism. But these isms are unfortunate caricatures, owing to our sins, our suspicions, and the lies of the devil. True holiness "is the most beautiful ornament and the most magnificent beauty which can be found in man."[5] Behold it in Christ and become like him in glory (2 Cor. 3:18).

God wants you to be holy. Through faith he already counts you holy in Christ. Now he intends to make you holy with Christ. This is no optional plan, no small potatoes. God saved you to sanctify you. God is in the beautification business, washing away spots and smoothing out wrinkles. He will have a blameless bride. He promises to work in you; he also calls you to work out. "The beauty of holiness" is first of all the Lord's (Ps. 29:2, kjv). But by his grace it can also be yours.

---

[5]Wilhelmus A Brakel, *The Christian's Reasonable Service*, trans. Bartel Elshout, ed. Joel R. Beeke, 4 vols. (Grand Rapids, MI: Reformation Heritage Books, 1994), 3:17.

STUDY QUESTIONS[1]

Chapter 1—Mind the Gap

1. What comes to mind when you hear the word "holiness"? Are your thoughts primarily positive? Negative? Encouraging? Discouraging? Burdensome? Freeing?

2. Growing up, how did your church, family, and friends speak of holiness?

3. Is the holiness of heaven a delightful thought for you? Does it equal the delight you have in thinking about heaven as a place of love, peace, enjoyment, and happiness? Why or why not?

4. Why does there appear to be a "hole in our holiness" today? Which of the reasons given by the author resonate with your own struggles with holiness?

5. What have been the major themes of your Christian life? Has holiness been one of those major themes?

Chapter 2—The Reason for Redemption

1. What reasons come to mind when you think about why God saved you?

2. What are some passages in Scripture that have impacted your life of holiness? Why do these hold significance?

3. Do you find the pursuit of holiness intimidating? Why or why not?

4. Does it seem disagreeable to stress personal holiness?

---

[1]These study questions have been contributed by Jason Helopoulos, a pastor with the Presbyterian Church in America.

Chapter 3 — Piety's Pattern

1. What assurance and confidence does definitive sanctification give?

2. Where has the church in previous generations gone wrong in its pursuit of holiness? What errors do you see today? Are some of them present in your own understanding of holiness?

3. As you read through the list of virtues and vices in this chapter, what are some of the vices in your life that you need to get rid of? What are some of the virtues you see and need to continue to encourage?

4. Of what things in your life would you have trouble saying, "I can thank God for this?"

5. Do you know the Ten Commandments? Do they shape your living? How?

Chapter 4 — The Impetus for the Imperatives

1. Do you delight in the law of the Lord? Do you see the law as an expression of God's grace? Why or why not?

2. What motivations for holiness listed in this chapter are currently the "best medicine" for you?

3. Which motivations for holiness have you seldom heard in sermons or within the church? Why do you think that is?

4. Think of a sin you are struggling with. Which biblical motivations for holiness provided in this chapter are an encouragement to you to pursue holiness and to mortify this sin?

Chapter 5 — The Pleasure of God and the Possibility of Godliness

1. Has your pursuit of personal holiness been short-circuited in certain ways? How?

2. When you are told that the Scriptures teach that righteousness is possible, that you truly can do good works, and you can please God, what is your reaction? Does it surprise you? Encourage you?

3. Do you allow yourself not only to be convicted while reading the Scriptures, listening to sermons, and reading Christian books, but also to be encouraged at the progress and "successes" within your Christian life?

Chapter 6—Sprit-powered, Gospel-driven, Faith-fueled Effort

1. Are there areas in your life where you have been resisting, grieving, or quenching the Spirit? What action do you need to take?

2. Do you remind yourself who you are in Christ? How does this encourage you in the pursuit of holiness?

3. What are some promises of God that are an encouragement to you?

4. Why does a "let go and let God" view of sanctification have a strong appeal? Why is it deadly to true growth in sanctification? Has your growth in sanctification been affected with this errant teaching? In what areas?

Chapter 7—Be Who You Are

1. Is union with Christ a new concept for you? If so, how might it change your view of sanctification? If you are already familiar with this idea, how has it already shaped your sanctification?

2. Is there a difference between aiming at something you're not and becoming something you are? How does this shape and motivate your pursuit of holiness?

3. Read through Romans 6. How would a life lived in knowledge of union with Christ be radically different from the lives of nonbelievers? Is being "in Christ" your identity?

Chapter 8—Saints and Sexual Immorality

1. Are you compromising in any area of your sensuality and sexuality? Do you see any evidence of a dulled conscience? Why have you been susceptible in this area?

2. What are some of the subtle or not so subtle influences in our culture propagating the idea that our bodies belong to us rather than to Christ?

3. Is there another area of your life in Christ in which sin has a foothold? How should union with Christ affect your obedience in this area?

Chapter 9—Abide and Obey

1. Does your view of life in Christ include the concepts of communion with Christ and obedience to Christ? How does each guide your living?

2. Is there a sin in your life that is currently disrupting your communion with Christ? How might a pursuit of prayer, Scripture, fellowship, and the Lord's Supper help you in your struggle with this sin?

3. Have you underestimated the channels of grace the Lord has given (i.e., prayer, Bible reading, the church, Lord's Table, etc.)?

Chapter 10—That All May See Your Progress

1. Who are some Christians you look up to in the faith? What marks their lives?

2. Would those closest to you (your spouse, children, friends, coworkers, parents) say that you have progressed in Christ over the past year? Ask them. Where do they see progress?

3. Look back over the past week. Where do you see moments of mere regret and where do you see moments of true repentance? What held you back from moving on to repentance in those moments of mere regret?

GENERAL INDEX

SCRIPTURE INDEX

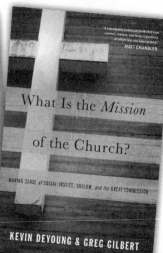

Also Available

from

KEVIN DEYOUNG

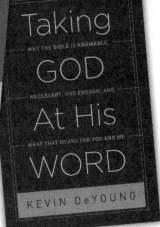